IN THIS ISSUE

PIVOT Magazine

Founder and President
Jason Miller

Editor-in-Chief
Chris O'Byrne

Design
JETLAUNCH.net

Advertising
Chris O'Byrne

Webmaster
Joel Phillips

Editor
Laura West

Cover Design
Debbie O'Byrne

Copyright © 2023 PIVOT

ISBN: 979-8-89079-068-2

LETTER FROM THE EDITOR

In this month's issue, we're thrilled to introduce you to Cassandra Scerbo, a force to be reckoned with in the realm of social impact, leadership, and creative enterprise. Known for her impressive acting career, Cassie wears multiple hats that go beyond the limelight. As the Vice President of Boo2Bullying, she has undertaken significant responsibilities that range from financial oversight to campaign development and event planning.

But why should business leaders and entrepreneurs pay attention to Cassie Scerbo? Because her endeavors in the nonprofit sector offer a masterclass in organizational management, strategy, and engagement.

Cassie Scerbo has successfully leveraged her platform to address pressing issues like bullying, and in doing so, she has demonstrated the qualities that embody effective leadership and management. As you read through her interview, you'll find valuable takeaways that can be applied not just to nonprofit management but also to the running of businesses in any sector.

We hope you find her insights as enlightening as we did.

Chris O'Byrne

FROM THE DESK OF THE PRESIDENT

Strategic Opportunities for Entrepreneurs in the Hollywood Film Industry

Hollywood is not just the epicenter of the film industry; it's a global cultural phenomenon that shapes narratives, influences trends, and generates billions of dollars annually. Hollywood's reach is broad and deep, from blockbuster hits that break box office records to critically acclaimed indie films that captivate niche audiences. Its economic power is evident in its ability to create vast employment opportunities, drive technological innovation, and even influence international trade by exporting American films and related merchandise.

For entrepreneurs, this dynamic landscape presents a plethora of opportunities. Whether you're interested in the creative aspects like scriptwriting and film production or more inclined towards the business facets like financing and distribution, there are multiple avenues to carve out a niche. There are many opportunities in the Hollywood film industry.

The Landscape of Hollywood Economics

Blockbuster films are the crown jewels of Hollywood, often raking in hundreds of millions, if not billions, of dollars globally. However, the path to such astronomical figures is paved with equally staggering costs and risks. Understanding the economics behind these big-ticket movies can offer entrepreneurs valuable insights into the industry's inner workings and potential entry points.

Budgeting

The budget of a blockbuster film is a complex puzzle divided into three main phases: pre-production, production, and post-production.

- **Pre-Production**: This phase involves script development, casting, and location scouting. Costs can range from a few hundred thousand to several million dollars.
- **Production**: The actual filming process is the most expensive part, involving costs for sets, crew salaries, and special effects. Budgets for this phase can easily exceed $100 million for blockbuster films.
- **Post-Production**: After filming, the movie enters the editing stage, followed by sound design, visual effects, and finally, marketing and distribution. This can add another tens of millions to the overall budget.

Financing

Financing a blockbuster is as intricate as its budgeting. Studios often bear the initial costs but look for additional revenue streams and risk mitigation strategies.

- **Studio Investment**: Major studios like Warner Bros. or Disney may self-finance their projects, but this is often a high-stakes gamble.
- **Co-Productions**: To spread the risk, studios frequently enter into co-production agreements with other companies, both domestic and international.
- **Investor Funding**: Private and institutional investors can also contribute, lured by the potential for high returns.

Return on Investment (ROI)

The ROI for blockbuster films can be phenomenal but is never guaranteed. Revenue streams are diversified to maximize the chances of profitability.

- **Box Office**: The most direct form of revenue, but also the riskiest due to market unpredictability.
- **Merchandising and Licensing**: These can often match or even exceed box office revenues, especially for franchise films.
- **Streaming and Syndication**: With the rise of streaming platforms, selling the rights to these services has become another lucrative avenue.

Understanding these components of Hollywood economics is crucial for entrepreneurs eyeing the film industry. Whether by offering specialized services in one of these areas, entering into partnerships, or even financing projects, the opportunities are as varied as they are abundant.

Technology-Driven Opportunities

Film Analytics Software

Market Need for Predictive Analytics

Predictive analytics can be a game-changer in an industry where the stakes are incredibly high. Studios invest enormous sums in film production and marketing, and the ability to predict a film's success can significantly mitigate risks. Analytics can offer insights into consumer behavior, market trends, and even predict box office performance based on variables like genre, star power, and release timing.

Example: Box Office Success Prediction Tool

Entrepreneurs can develop software that uses machine learning algorithms to analyze historical box office data, social media buzz, and other relevant metrics. This tool could give studios a predictive analysis of a film's potential success, helping them make informed decisions on marketing spend, release dates, and distribution strategies.

Virtual Reality Studios

The Rise of VR in Film Experiences

Virtual Reality (VR) is no longer just a buzzword; it's becoming an integral part of the film industry. From VR film festivals to immersive experiences that complement traditional films, the technology offers a new layer of engagement and revenue streams. Studios are increasingly interested in VR to extend the lifecycle of a film, offering fans new ways to interact with their favorite characters and storylines.

Example: VR Add-Ons for Blockbuster Films

Entrepreneurs can capitalize on this trend by creating VR studios specializing in developing immersive experiences tied to blockbuster releases. Imagine a VR experience that lets fans explore the fictional world of a popular film, interact with its characters, or even influence the storyline. These VR add-ons can be sold separately or bundled with movie tickets, providing a unique selling proposition for your VR studio and an additional revenue channel for studios.

By tapping into the technological trends shaping the film industry, entrepreneurs can position themselves at the forefront of innovation, offering services that enhance the movie-going experience and provide valuable data-driven insights to studios.

Marketing and Branding Avenues

Influencer Partnerships

The Power of Social Media in Film Promotion

Social media has revolutionized how films are marketed, offering a more direct and interactive channel to reach audiences. With their extensive and often highly engaged followings, influencers have become invaluable partners in film promotion. Their endorsements can generate buzz, drive ticket sales, and even influence a film's public perception.

Example: Influencer-Led Campaigns for Film Releases

Entrepreneurs can create agencies specializing in connecting influencers with film studios for promotional campaigns. For instance, influencers who specialize in fitness or adventure sports could promote an action movie, offering authentic endorsements that resonate with their followers. These campaigns can include exclusive previews, behind-the-scenes content, or even interactive Q&A sessions, providing a multi-layered promotional strategy beyond traditional advertising.

Film Merchandising

Licensing and Revenue Potential

Merchandising is a significant revenue stream that can often rival or even surpass box office earnings, especially for franchise films. The possibilities are endless, from toys and apparel to video games and home decor. Licensing agreements allow studios to monetize their intellectual property while manufacturers get to produce goods for an established and eager market.

Example: Creating Merchandise for Superhero Movies

Entrepreneurs can enter this space by acquiring licensing rights to create and sell movie-related merchandise. For example, if you secure the rights for a popular superhero movie, you could produce a range of products, from action figures to themed clothing. These items can be sold online, in specialty stores, or even directly through partnerships with movie theaters, creating multiple channels for revenue.

Entrepreneurs can tap into the immense promotional power needed to make a film successful by focusing on marketing and branding avenues. Whether it's through social media campaigns or merchandising, these strategies offer a win-win situation: studios get to amplify their reach and revenue while entrepreneurs carve out a lucrative niche in the Hollywood ecosystem.

Financial Involvement and Risk Mitigation

Film Financing

Types of Financing and Risk Factors

Financing a film is a complex endeavor that involves multiple sources of capital. The most common types include:

- **Equity Financing**: Direct investment into the film project, usually in exchange for a share of the profits.
- **Debt Financing**: Loans secured against the film's future earnings or other assets.
- **Grants and Subsidies**: Non-repayable funds usually provided by

government agencies or foundations.

Each type of financing comes with its own set of risks, such as market unpredictability, over-budgeting, or even legal complications related to intellectual property.

Example: Creating a Film Investment Fund

Entrepreneurs with financial acumen can create a specialized film investment fund that pools capital from various investors to finance multiple film projects. This diversification can mitigate risks and increase the chances of a profitable return. The fund can also specialize in certain types of films, such as indie projects or specific genres, to leverage market gaps and expertise.

Tax Credit Brokering

How Tax Incentives Work and Their Value

Many countries and states offer tax incentives to encourage film production within their jurisdictions. These incentives can take the form of tax credits, rebates, or even exemptions. They can significantly reduce the overall cost of a film project, making them highly valuable to studios.

Example: Facilitating Tax Credits for Studios

Entrepreneurs can act as brokers or consultants, helping studios navigate the complex landscape of tax incentives. This could involve identifying the most lucrative tax credits available, assisting with the application process, and even selling or trading tax credits between different entities. Your firm could charge a fee or a percentage of the tax savings, creating a win-win scenario for both parties.

By engaging in financial involvement and risk mitigation strategies, entrepreneurs can offer valuable services that address some of the film industry's most pressing challenges. Whether through innovative financing models or leveraging tax incentives, these avenues provide a fertile ground for entrepreneurs to grow and succeed in Hollywood.

The Hollywood film industry presents a multifaceted landscape ripe with opportunities for entrepreneurs. From content creation and technology-driven solutions to marketing strategies and financial involvement, the avenues for entry are diverse. Each offers its own set of challenges and rewards, but all hold the promise of significant impact. Niche and novel opportunities like film tourism and specialized film festivals further expand the entrepreneurial landscape, allowing for creative and unique business ventures.

Success in the film industry requires more than just a good idea; it demands a strategic approach. Entrepreneurs should start by identifying gaps in the market or underserved needs within the industry. Once a niche is identified, the next steps involve meticulous planning, from securing financing to building a competent team.

It's also crucial to stay updated on industry trends, as the film business is ever-evolving. Whether it's the rise of streaming platforms, changes in consumer behavior, or even shifts in international markets, being ahead of the curve can offer a competitive advantage.

Lastly, networking cannot be overstated. The film industry is built on relationships. Attend industry events, seek mentorship from industry veterans, and don't underestimate the power of a well-placed introduction.

By combining market insight with strategic planning and effective networking, entrepreneurs can enter and thrive in Hollywood's competitive yet rewarding world.

AN INTERVIEW WITH CASSIE SCERBO, HOLLYWOOD ACTRESS AND ADVOCATE FOR BOO2BULLYING

Chris O'Byrne:

Hi, Cassie. Can you share a significant childhood experience that shaped who you are today?

Cassie Scerbo

That's a great question. Many of my friends have actually held inner-child workshops recently. The main purpose is to reveal where certain patterns or emotions may stem from and to reflect on your younger self. What's funny, is I found the opposite to be more interesting in my case, as I often wonder what advice my younger self would give me now! As a child, I was extremely headstrong, vivacious, and passionate. I had a very colorful childhood, filled with too many wonderful experiences to name, all of them shaping the person I am today. From family vacations, to living out my dreams. Every mistake I've made, I've tried to learn from and all of the great memories, I cherish.

Throughout my thirty-three-year life, I've always had a natural love for performing. And have always considered myself to be a "people person." I had begged my parents since I could talk to take acting, dancing, and singing classes. Seeing smiles on people's faces and feeling like I contributed to that happiness brought me great joy. At around ten years old, I started auditioning in Miami, and my mother graciously supported me by shuttling me back and forth from Parkland to Miami for every casting call, whether for commercials or modeling gigs.

Regarding my career, I've always been determined and never had a plan B. I didn't believe in having backup plans as a child. I always said, "This is what I want to do, and I will make it happen." When I was fourteen, I went to LA for the first time. Fun fact, it was for a screen test for *Hannah Montana*. I'm incredibly happy for Miley; she's amazing! Although I didn't get that role, it didn't discourage me. Instead, I became

even more eager, excited, and grateful for the connections I had made. I continued working with Disney and on many different projects, and the rest is history. I genuinely love what I do. So, to answer your question about how my childhood shaped who I am today, I can ultimately say that I was always passionate and had a mindset of never giving up, as cliché as that may sound. This mindset granted me so many wonderful opportunities I can only thank my younger self for!

I am also fortunate to have a very supportive family all-around. Being in this industry at a young age can be challenging for a family. My mom would bring me back and forth to LA, and my parents have remained together through it all. We constantly flew back to Florida, or my father and siblings would fly out to visit us in LA. Their support, both emotionally and financially, is something I am incredibly grateful for and never take for granted.

Their love and affection were crucial as a child pursuing this type of work, with all the flights and traveling. It fueled me and helped me stay on my path, especially considering the amount of rejection in this industry. Having thick skin and a support system is essential.

Looking back, I realize that even as a child, I possessed an extreme amount of determination. Life

can become tougher sometimes as you grow older but truly believing in myself and having that support has been invaluable.

Chris O'Byrne

Breaking into the acting industry can be very challenging and requires a great deal of persistence and determination. How persistent do you have to be?

Cassie Scerbo

Very persistent. Every individual's journey in the acting industry is unique. For some, success may come quickly, with rare breakthroughs and landing significant roles immediately. My first taste of the acting world was when I was booked as an extra in a Burger King commercial. I wasn't a featured extra or anything like that, just a background presence. If I recall correctly, I was dressed in karate gear for that commercial. It's been a while, so the details are a bit fuzzy, but I remember feeling so incredibly excited about that role.

It's exhilarating for a child to be on a set, surrounded by cameras and immersed in the place they've always dreamt of. For me, it took some time to make progress in the industry. However, with each job, my passion grew stronger, and my desire to succeed intensified alongside the trials and obstacles

I faced. I believe I'm the kind of person who thrives on challenges. I enjoy proving others wrong and breaking out of the stereotypes associated with certain roles. Today, it's about defying expectations and embracing new opportunities.

However, during my younger years, my primary drive was to prove to myself that I could achieve this dream. Honestly, I never had any doubt. I didn't. I firmly believe that mindset plays a vital role in achieving success. It's about visualizing, imagining, and wholeheartedly believing in one's aspirations, manifesting them into reality. Undoubtedly, it's not an easy path, but the rewards are 100% worth it. I firmly believe that all the challenges I've faced in the industry have only deepened my love and passion for it.

Chris O'Byrne

What were some of the low points or struggles you encountered?

Cassie Scerbo

In the entertainment industry, anyone, I'm not just referring to myself, can possess immense talent and be an exceptional actor, right? But often, it boils down to timing or a specific appearance that fits that project's requirements. There are countless reasons why things may not go as planned. That

can be frustrating because, in other professions, you can go to school, put in hard work, and gradually climb the ladder. It's not as unpredictable and volatile as the entertainment industry. Our industry doesn't necessarily have a set path or specific steps to follow. Sometimes, it's all about timing. Other times, hard work aligns with the right opportunity.

There's a quote that speaks to the truth of this. It's along the lines that persistence combined with the right opportunity or crossing paths with someone who genuinely believes in your talent can make all the difference. You never know what might happen.

However, there are certain steps to take to reach that point, and it's not always within your control or solely dependent on your talent, hard work, or the number of classes you take. You may not

land a role or book something in the industry for countless reasons. The most challenging moments are when I'm not working because on set is where I feel happiest. It's my happy place. Additionally, another challenge I face is being stereotyped. I've dealt with it throughout my life, and I constantly strive to break down those stereotypes.

That's another challenge to add to the list. Numerous challenges come with being in the industry. Hollywood is a fast-paced and intense town filled with countless individuals who share the same goals and dreams. It creates a highly competitive environment where standing out and making a mark can be quite challenging. As I mentioned, finding your tribe and having a strong support system are essential. It's important to check in with yourself often and prioritize your mental health as well. I strongly believe in the significance of mental health check-ins, and it's a topic I frequently advocate for. This aligns perfectly with my work with my nonprofit organization, Boo2Bullying, where we strive to combat bullying and promote mental well-being.

There's a massive parallel between bullying and mental health, whether it involves someone else bullying you or even self-bullying. We emphasize the importance of perseverance, continuously advocating for yourself, and supporting those around you. It's crucial to champion both your well-being and the well-being of others to create a positive and supportive environment.

The entertainment industry is incredibly tough, filled with numerous challenging moments due to its unpredictable nature. One day, you may feel like you're on top of the mountain while working on a project, but six months later, you might struggle to secure a job or book new opportunities. The ups and downs can be emotionally and mentally demanding, requiring resilience and perseverance to navigate the industry's fluctuating landscape. Despite the occasional struggle to book jobs, I feel blessed to have worked solely in the industry and engaged in meaningful charity work.

However, many people are tirelessly working multiple jobs on the side, such as Uber driving, bartending, or waitressing. It's a tough industry, but if you want it bad enough, you have to stick it out!

Chris O'Byrne

I've always wanted to know, what is the business side of being an actor like?

Cassie Scerbo

If we're not talking about the business side when it comes to

agents, managers, and lawyers, your primary focus should be perfecting your craft as an actor. This entails staying dedicated to taking classes, which can often be quite costly.

The main thing is consistently putting yourself out there to the best of your ability. I believe for many actors, exploring other creative outlets is also important. I'm currently venturing into producing myself. I aspire to write and direct in the future as well, but I prioritize keeping myself busy and attending classes whenever possible. I understand that there can be challenges for some people. I've been fortunate enough to have the opportunity to remain in classes throughout my career and collaborate with some incredible coaches. Overall, for actors, it boils down to continuously sharpening those tools in the toolbox and staying on point with what you love to do.

There are also other small things, like ensuring you have current headshots. Nowadays, with the prevalence of social media, it's fundamental to stay connected with fans and continuously release content. I guess that's more reflective of the new world we live in. But as an actor, your primary responsibility is to persistently pursue what you love and refine your craft. This might sound simple, but engaging in workshops, attending masterclasses, and working with such incredible coaches can be,

once again, intense experiences and costly.

That's the reality of it. You're really digging in. Acting is like psychology in a sense. It involves getting to know how the human brain works. Then, it's about taking that knowledge and applying it whenever you step into a new role. How does the character think? It doesn't matter who that character may be. It involves journaling and conducting an extensive amount of research.

If you're playing a doctor, you need to research to make sure you carry yourself like a doctor would, speak like a doctor and know how to properly hold the tools that a doctor/surgeon would hold etc.

Chris O'Byrne

There are a lot of similarities with entrepreneurs as well. They, too, have creative outlets and must focus on their craft to be successful. Like actors, entrepreneurs must understand what they do and constantly work on improving their skills. Additionally, both actors and entrepreneurs must balance creating content and ensuring it aligns with their goals and target audience, which is difficult.

Cassie Scerbo

It has been difficult to navigate this new digital landscape, especially for someone like me, who started acting before the era of social media. When I went out to Los Angeles, my goal was to become an actress—not an influencer. Years ago, I ventured into acting because of my deep love for it. I loved embodying these different characters, researching, understanding people in general, connecting with people, and performing.

It can be hard to feel the pressure to constantly produce content and stay relevant to keep up with the times. While I have all the respect in the world for people who are influencers and enjoy scrolling through social media and watching people's dances or "get ready with me" videos, it's not where my personal passion lies.

However, I'm working on improving this because I also want to continue giving my fans and supporters—though I must admit, the word "fans" makes me feel a bit uncomfortable—the best experience possible. I'm grateful for the support I have received, whether it's from longtime supporters or new fans and I want to be able to provide them with more content and connect with them as much as possible.

I'm still learning to effectively navigate and improve my content creation, making it more conducive to my lifestyle. It's important to remember that everyone's approach to content creation is unique and varies greatly.

I'm exploring my existing passions, such as cooking, and considering posting more videos about it. Filming at home is easier, where I can simply set up the camera and do my thing. On the other hand, I prefer not to constantly record everything when I'm out with loved ones, trying to enjoy our time together. It's a new world, a new age, and I'm doing my best to adapt and provide my supporters with more content consistently.

Creating content is like having a job on its own. Between auditions (when not on strike), charity work as vice president of Boo2Bullying and trying to find time for my personal life, it's challenging to prioritize content creation. However, I'm doing my best to provide my social media followers as much as possible. It's important to always set boundaries and to live in the moment, travel, and enjoy time with your loved ones as well.

Chris O'Byrne

Who have been some of the key influences or mentors in your life?

Cassie Scerbo

I have many in the different aspects of my life, particularly my family members, who are all immensely talented and influential. They have a positive impact on my life. Certain acting coaches have become my biggest mentors, witnessing my vulnerability and providing valuable guidance in pursuing the thing I love most in this world.

Additionally, I'm fortunate to have some incredible friends both within and outside the industry who I greatly admire.

I've encountered various mentors, including strangers and activists, who have inspired me beyond belief. It's difficult to pinpoint a specific source of inspiration because I believe even encounters with strangers on the street can be enlightening. I strive to learn from as many remarkable individuals as possible.

Chris O'Byrne

I agree with your point about finding inspiration in strangers. It's all about having the mindset of seeking inspiration in everyone you encounter.

Cassie Scerbo

Absolutely! I had a conversation with my dental hygienist, Sandy, today, and I found her exceptionally inspiring. She's currently working on an amazing book. It's important to seek inspiration from everyone you meet.

It's true that what you seek is often what you'll find. I believe in the power of gratitude and putting positive energy into the world as much as possible.

Chris O'Byrne

What do you do as the vice president for Boo2Bullying?

Cassie Scerbo

That's a long list as well. As the vice president, my responsibilities include financial oversight, collaborating with school districts, developing creative campaigns, and handling event planning. I also actively participate in committees for events, coordinating with our dedicated event committee through frequent communication, attend school assemblies, speak on panels, and contribute to budgeting efforts.

Additionally, I assist with social media management by collaborating with our social media manager to brainstorm creative ways to engage and support people through various online platforms.

As vice president, alongside our president Dimitri Halkidas, our focus includes being leaders, supporting our board members and ambassadors, attending events and parades, and passionately promoting and fulfilling our organization's mission statement.

Chris O'Byrne

What does Boo2Bullying do?

Cassie Scerbo

Boo2Bullying is a 501(c)(3) organization celebrating its tenth anniversary. Our main focus is conducting school assemblies to address bullying. We strive to create a safe environment where students can share their stories and concerns. Before each assembly, we communicate with teachers and administration to understand the specific challenges and climate of the school. We recognize that every school and grade level faces unique bullying issues, and our goal is to provide a safe space for discussion and support.

Another important thing we strive to teach is that vulnerability is a superpower.

We emphasize the importance of honesty, openness, and standing up for others instead of being bystanders. We also believe self-love plays a crucial role in addressing bullying issues.

We also address the concept of self-bullying, which is the opposite of self-love. Self-love is about accepting oneself—flaws and all—rather than striving for perfection. It involves recognizing areas for improvement while also acknowledging and celebrating personal achievements.

We focus on various forms of bullying including anti-Semitism, racism, and supporting the LGBTQIA+ community. Boo2Bullying is also committed to suicide prevention efforts.

We are also involved in teaching young children through two programs for grades K–3 that aim to instill foundational values and promote kindness. Sometimes, life's challenges can make it difficult to maintain these principles. The first program is called "Cape Nation", and it stands for Courage, Appreciate, Personal Health, and Education. It's all about emphasizing that anybody can be a superhero. The second program, "Parker and Boo", is an animated short film we produced alongside Danimation, who created all the animation for this wonderful short we did. I voice Parker, while Rob Paulson, known for iconic roles such as Pinky and the Brain, Jimmy

Neutron, and the Ninja Turtles, voices Boo, our mascot.

It's about finding ways to teach children from a very young age how to eradicate hate and intolerance in a way they understand.

We primarily conduct school assemblies but also engage in outreach and provide support to people in need. Bullying can take many forms and affect people at different levels, so it's important to equip kids and teens with the necessary tools to combat bullying.

Chris O'Byrne

As an example, how can you help a middle-school bully change their behavior?

Cassie Scerbo

It's crucial to understand the underlying reasons for their actions to help a middle school bully change their behavior. Happy, supported people who have self-love don't typically engage in bullying. Therefore, it's important to uncover the root cause behind their behavior.

After speaking at schools, students often approach us to share that they have been bullying, and they often attribute it to what they've witnessed at home. Understanding the root cause of their behavior is crucial. While I'm not a psychologist, I

have a knack for understanding people and enjoy helping them uncover their underlying issues.

If I suspect a student requires counseling or is in an unsafe home environment, I make sure to connect them with appropriate resources. I also advise students experiencing bullying or engaging in it due to personal struggles to seek help and have conversations about their experiences. Breaking the silence and expressing oneself can save lives and prevent negativity from festering in isolation.

The most important thing when struggling, whether as a bully or bullied, is to not bottle up emotions. Find someone or an organization you trust to talk to, like Boo2Bullying. Speak up and stand up for yourself. Focus on passions and hobbies to distract from negativity. Stay positive and pursue what you love.

Chris O'Byrne

That was a lot of great advice. I appreciate that. To conclude, what parting words of guidance would you like to share?

Cassie Scerbo

One quote I love is, "No one outside of you can make you feel inferior without your consent." It's a powerful reminder to love and accept yourself. Loving yourself is essential because it allows you to love life and others

fully. It may not always be easy, especially during times of self-doubt, but those are the moments you need to love yourself the most. By championing yourself and getting back on track, you can continue doing what you love and love others properly. Self-love is incredibly important; if everyone could embrace it, the world would be better.

I hope people don't read this and think, *There's that word again* or *#Selflove*. But at the end of the day, it means acceptance. It's accepting whatever has happened, whatever you've been through, whatever isn't feeling good. It's okay to not always be okay. You're not alone in what you're going through. There are over seven billion people on this planet. Surround yourself with the right people, speak up, and get these negative feelings out of your body. Therapy can be helpful, too. I believe in breaking stigmas and think anyone can benefit from simply speaking negative feelings and emotions out of their body.

About the Author

Best known for her acting resume having already led various TV series and films including Freeform's *Make it or Break it*, the *Sharknado* film series, *Truth or Dare* on Netflix, ABC's *Grand Hotel* and Neil LaBute's *Bench Seat*, as well as garnering accolades such as People's Choice Awards and Teen Choice Awards nominations and a Telly Awards win for her recent segment on CBS's *Wake up with Marci*.

Most importantly, Cassie is an advocate against bullying. First joining as a girl's youth ambassador almost fifteen years ago, Cassie has risen to be the Vice President of Boo2Bullying, a nonprofit seeking to eradicate bullying, intolerance, and discrimination by educating schools and parents about accepting diversity and giving young people the proper tools to connect with and positively impact those around them. In addition to speaking on panels and in schools against bullying, Cassie regularly holds fundraisers to raise money for their educational programs and suicide prevention outreach.

As a former student of Marjory Stoneman Douglas High School in Parkland, FL who was deeply affected by the tragic school shooting, Cassie helped executive-produce the newly released documentary, *Code Red: Youth of the Nation*, currently available to watch on Amazon Prime Video, Apple TV, Google Play, YouTube, etc. From the most influential young voices of America, *Code Red: Youth of the Nation* searches and finds the answers of how we can protect our most vulnerable from the greatest threats of their generation. From COVID-19 and mental health, education policy and school safety, Code Red uses the deadliest high school massacre in American history at Marjory Stoneman Douglas High School in Parkland, Florida as a vehicle to experientially illustrate and engage through the testimonies of the FBI, students, teachers, law enforcement and SWAT commanders, psychologists and education experts of how we, as parents, teachers and students, have the ability to act and avoid a #generationlost.

Born on the east coast in Long Island, New York with a large traditional Italian family, and later moving to Parkland, FL, Cassie began taking her first dance lessons at the young age of four and immediately knew she wanted to be a performer. By age ten, Cassie had an agent in South Florida and had began booking commercial and print work. She then went on to split her time between Los Angeles and Florida while pursuing her dream. As a teenager, Cassie was signed to Geffen Records and DIC Entertainment as one of five girls chosen by veteran music producer/executive Ron Fair for the girl group Slumber Party Girls (SPG), who began appearing on the Saturday morning CBS TV series *Dance Revolution*. From there, Cassie continued to hone her skills as an actor and landed the role as one of the leads in *Bring It On: In It to Win it*, starring opposite Ashley Benson.

In her free time, Cassie can be found at her local boxing gym, traveling, cooking, or finding any reason to go to South Florida to visit her family.

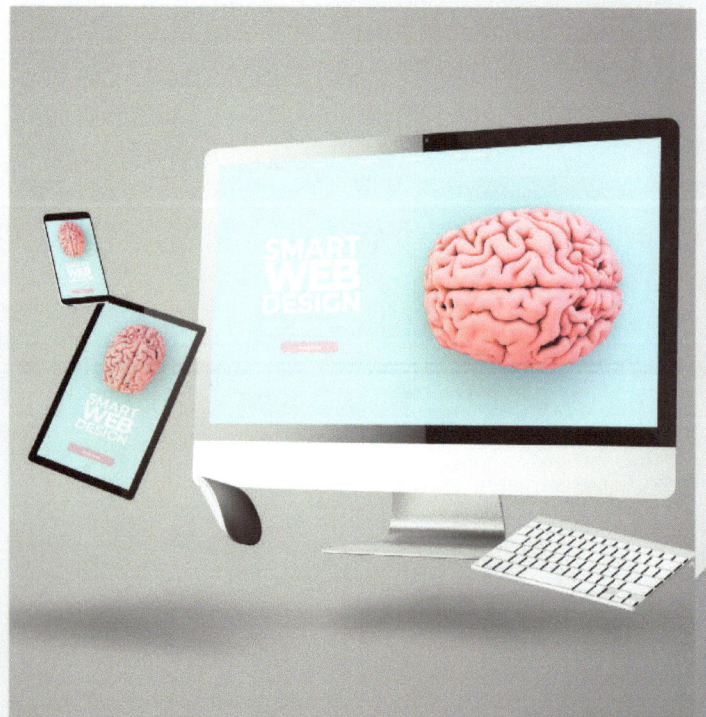

LESSONS IN INTEGRITY AND MINDFULNESS FROM A NAVY SEAL

JON MACASKILL

Chris O'Byrne

What's a childhood story that influenced who you became today?

Jon Macaskill

One childhood story that influenced me was when I was part of the track and cross-country teams in high school in Ruston, Louisiana. After a particularly successful race, my father and I went to pick up the newspaper the next day. I eagerly grabbed multiple copies to share the news with my mom and friends. This experience taught me the value of hard work and the importance of celebrating achievements, even before the internet era.

I returned to the car with the stack of ten papers. My dad looked at me, questioning my actions. I explained that I had paid 25 cents for the newspapers. He responded by putting nine more quarters in for the newspapers

I had essentially stolen. This incident taught me the value of integrity and has shaped who I am today. It was a turning point in my life, making me realize the dishonesty I'd been getting away with. My dad's words about giving away everything except integrity have guided my work ethic and desire to give back.

Chris O'Byrne

It speaks volumes about your character that you recognized the significance of the situation instead of dismissing it and thinking you could get away with it the next time your dad wasn't around. When did you decide to join the military and aim for the SEALs?

Jon Macaskill

I developed a desire to serve at a young age, but it became stronger when I started running track and cross country. I noticed some of my teammates came from disadvantaged backgrounds, living in homes without proper floors or foundations. This further motivated me to serve in some capacity.

I recognized the potential in my teammates to change their lives through running, so I would give them rides to and from practice. Our close-knit group became successful in the running world, going undefeated for two seasons and winning state championships twice. I wanted to be part of a

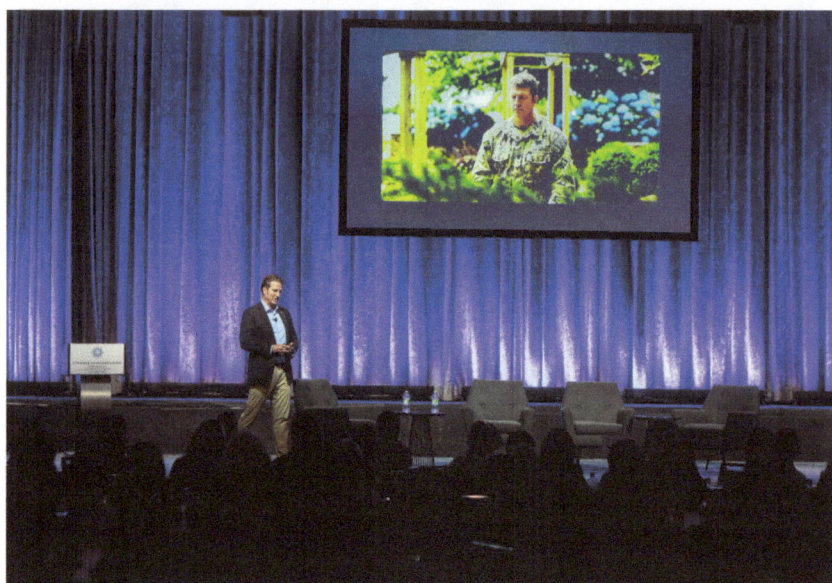

larger, elite group and continue serving, which led me to consider the military as an opportunity.

The tight-knit brotherhood within the Special Operations community and the Navy SEALs specifically appealed to me due to my love for the water. Growing up, I spent most of my time in or around the ocean during summer vacations. This made pursuing a career as a Navy SEAL within the Special Operations community the top choice for me. That's essentially the origin story of my journey into Special Operations.

Chris O'Byrne

Did you join right out of high school?

Jon Macaskill

I did. I initially tried to enter the Naval Academy after high school but was rejected. Determined to

still join the Navy, I enlisted and later was accepted into the Naval Academy from the enlisted ranks. I had also applied for Navy SEALs training but received acceptance to the academy first, leading me to choose that path. After graduating in 2001, I entered the SEAL training pipeline and became a Navy SEAL a few years later.

Chris O'Byrne

Do you have a story that stands out about getting to where you are in business now?

Jon Macaskill

In 2005, I was involved in Operation Red Wings. Though I was initially supposed to be on the ground, circumstances led me to be in the operations center instead. This operation, famously known for the lone survivor story of Marcus Luttrell, resulted in the loss of three men on the ground and sixteen operators. Among them were eight SEALs and eight Army Night Stalkers. Tragically, an RPG also shot down a helicopter, resulting in a total of nineteen men lost.

After being pulled off the operation, I found myself in the operation center, taking calls during the firefight that followed the downed helicopter. I felt an overwhelming sense of survivor guilt, questioning why I deserved to live while these brave men, whom I considered better than myself, perished. They were husbands, fathers, and brothers, embodying everything I was and more. The guilt, shared by many others, led to anxiety and depression for me.

I turned to alcohol and prescription medications to cope, reaching a dark point where I needed help. Through counseling, I was introduced to mindfulness and meditation, which, skeptically, changed and saved my life. Now, I teach these practices as a performance enhancer and as a means of finding peace and fulfillment. It's my duty to share these life-changing practices with others, as they were shared with me, hoping to change and save more lives.

Chris O'Byrne

Who are some mentors who influenced you along the way?

Jon Macaskill

I host the *Men Talking Mindfulness* podcast with my friend Will Schneider, a yoga practitioner and mindfulness teacher. Will has been a mentor to me on my mindfulness journey. Dr. Theresa Lawson, whom you've met, inspires me in her daily practice of mindfulness, meditation, and overall wellness. Sometimes, mindfulness can involve movement, which is connected to it.

Another mindfulness practitioner I want to mention is Neil Markey, a former Army Ranger who left the service to pursue his passion. He now runs an organization that teaches mindfulness and meditation to special operators and anyone seeking peace and fulfillment. I could mention many more names, but let's move on for now.

Chris O'Byrne

There are quite a few people who are teaching mindfulness and meditation. What's unique about what you do and your approach?

Jon Macaskill

There is a great need for more mindfulness teachers. Just like we need many good teachers for our young children, the stress and anxiety in today's world, with constant access to information and overwhelming responsibilities, calls for more support.

We need more teachers who specialize in mindfulness and meditation, especially for veterans, first responders, and C-suite executives. Many current teachers may not have the background that resonates with these groups.

My background allows me to connect with C-suite executives, veterans, and first responders in a unique way. This connection enables me to effectively communicate the message of mindfulness and meditation to these groups.

Chris O'Byrne

Yes, that makes a lot of sense. Do you have any success stories of helping busy, burned-out CEOs or executives?

Jon Macaskill

A former classmate from the Naval Academy approached me a couple of years ago. He was the president and CEO of a multimillion-dollar company, feeling overwhelmed and burned out. He wanted to find a solution not only for himself but also for his team members who were facing similar challenges.

He invited Theresa and me to work with his organization initially. After attending a workshop, he immediately signed up for our retreat, where we teach mindfulness, movement, and yoga. Since then, he has undergone a remarkable transformation. While he still faces challenges such as anxiety, stress, and burnout, mindfulness meditation has given him the tools to handle those difficulties better. It's like having a variety of tools in a toolbox instead of relying solely on a hammer.

He continues to seek our guidance, and we maintain an ongoing working relationship with him and his company. He's expressed that our teachings have transformed him and his relationships with his spouse and children. Moreover, it has profoundly impacted his organization, resulting in a significant increase in their bottom line over the past year and a half. This success story is just one example among several others we are proud of.

Chris O'Byrne

It's important to note that practicing mindfulness and incorporating these techniques can have practical financial benefits beyond simply feeling better. It has the potential to positively impact your bottom line and yield tangible results.

Jon Macaskill

Absolutely, it can. When pitching mindfulness to the C-suite, I highlight potential financial benefits. However, I'm also aware that implementing these practices can lead to a happier, healthier, more fulfilled workforce, resulting in reduced turnover rates and less absenteeism. By positively influencing the culture within an organization, the potential for increased financial success naturally follows.

Chris O'Byrne

Looking back on your entrepreneurial journey, what is one of your most important lessons?

Jon Macaskill

The most important lesson I've learned is that the entrepreneurial journey is unpredictable and full of ups and downs. Each day is unique, and my plans can be easily disrupted.

Entrepreneurship is a roller coaster ride, both financially

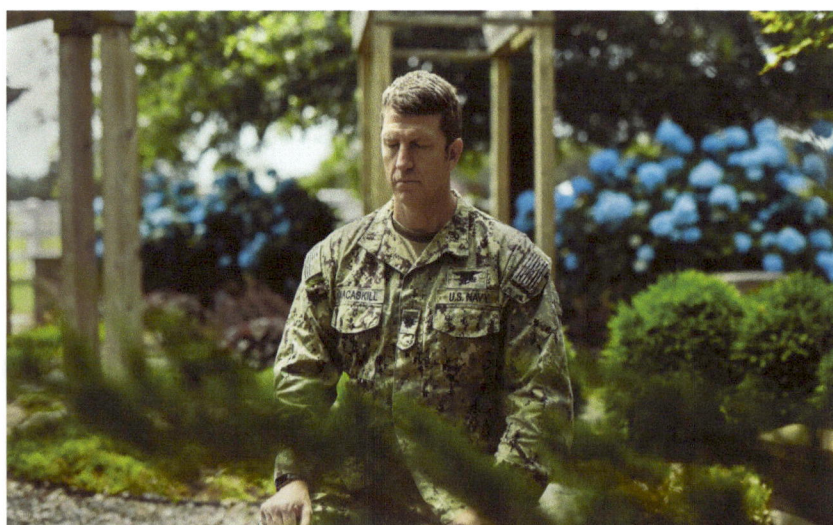

and emotionally. There are highs and lows in terms of finances, making strategies, and sales funnel optimization. If you expect a steady and smooth journey, entrepreneurship may not be the right path for you. In my experience, there are always surprises and unexpected twists along the way.

Chris O'Byrne

And the mindfulness and meditation is probably one of the best ways to prepare for those days. Do you have a typical morning routine?

Jon Macaskill

Yes, sometimes my children can impact my morning routine, but ideally, I wake up and take care of my basic needs before dedicating fifteen to thirty minutes to meditation. I often practice Wim Hof breathing as part of my meditation routine.

I begin my morning routine with a calming meditation to relax my nervous system. Then, I transition into Wim Hof breathing to energize and focus myself. After that, I engage in some form of moderate physical exercise, avoiding intense workouts.

After my morning exercise routine, I take a cold shower, enjoy a cup of coffee, and have breakfast before starting my day. In the afternoon, I incorporate non-sleep deep relaxation (NSDR), which involves

meditation. I typically practice yoga for fifteen to twenty minutes to deeply relax and reset my brain and nervous system for the rest of the day.

After my afternoon relaxation session, I feel recharged and ready to spend time with my energetic kids in the evening. This is how my morning routine and daily meditation practice help me maintain the energy I need throughout the day.

Chris O'Byrne

Do you have any parting words of wisdom?

Jon Macaskill

Be mindful and practice meditation. These terms may be buzzwords, but the more people hear about them, the more they will be accepted.

Do your research and understand the science behind mindfulness and meditation. It is not just woo-woo; there are physiological changes happening in your brain and body. It can improve your mind, soul, and emotions. There is proof that it can change the way you feel, perform, and interact with others. It can have a powerful impact on your personal and professional life.

Give mindfulness and meditation a chance. Research why and how it works, then try it out for yourself.

About the Author

Jon Macaskill (pronounced Muh-KAS-kill) is a retired Navy SEAL Commander turned mindfulness teacher and leadership coach. During his twenty-four-year Navy career, he served in multiple highly dynamic leadership positions, from the battlefield to the operations center and the board room. Jon's unconventional yet highly effective style of teaching leadership is fueled by his passion for helping people and organizations become the best versions of themselves. He takes what helped him excel in his professional life and heal in his personal life and now shares this through mindfulness coaching, grit and resilience training, and keynote speaking, all in the pursuit of helping others achieve their full potential. Learn more at frogmanmindfulness.com.

NONPROFIT OF THE MONTH: THE FLORIDA ASSOCIATION OF VETERAN-OWNED BUSINESSES

WILL BLACK

"It's not really a Chamber of Commerce," says Stu Smith of the Florida Association of Veteran-Owned Businesses. Mind you, Florida alone has something north of 187,000 veteran-owned businesses. Read that again—187 *thousand*. "We don't want to take away from Chambers but would rather stay in our lane. Our specialty is networking these men and women with each other."

With 5 chapters and 450+ members they are growing fast and have the businesses to do so. In 2020, $1 million in business went between just 63 of these vets' companies in work they shared with each other. There are groups that like to say they eat their own dog food, meaning, they don't just say what to do, but do it themselves every day. $1 million in contracts going back and forth in a community of vets is not just eating your own dog food, it's then eating the whole damn can it came in.

"We made a very conscious decision *not* to label ourselves as a Chamber of Commerce. We don't want to compete against our fellow chambers. We want to be a business association. We don't want to have an incubator. Our core competency is networking and connections. We want to be the recognized voice for veteran-owned businesses in Florida to position the state as the number one state of choice to own and operate a business."

Stu is no stranger to the work. He put in his hours. Two enlistments of about seven years in the service and he was recognized in 1987 as the 9th Infantry Division, I Corps and FORSCOM *Soldier of the Year*. A corporate career path in training and development eventually led to Human Resources where he was hired by an Atlanta firm as his "last paid job."

" I went from helping veterans get the benefits they wanted to helping my fellow veterans get employed because I was in the HR field."

God's own providence led to a chance meeting where he would be brought into the mere seven-year-old FAVOB where he would come in as the secretary, then vice chair, then chair of a Chapter. In Stu's own words, he was getting ready to "play golf more often than work". But the founder asked Stu if he could help him out and in April of 2022, he took the CEO role for all of FAVOB.

They also have a standard nonprofit arm as a 501c3 to boot. This allows them to do and help even more, while opening them to greater funding opportunities. In researching FAVOB, I spoke to other chapters, and I know the tight, lean ship they run. FAVOB doesn't waste a nickel. They run entire chapters on the average allowance given to a 13-year-old who can barely do a decent job cutting the grass, and they serve hundreds of members on it.

I didn't get it. Some groups I speak to have the budget of a small nation's military. How do they do it? Everyone's a volunteer and they get as much as possible donated for any event they have. It's amazing. What would they do with an extra $100k in donations?

The next step is the marketplace for the veterans and their

businesses, along with the GIS (geographic information system) and the talent and technology to put it to real work. FAVOB's connection of businesses to other people and resources they need sometimes borders on the mystic when it's really just hard work. Getting people in front of the contracts, the systems, and other groups looking for their specific skillsets is where Stu and FAVOB shine. His past experience of helping organize groups really pays off in his work at FAVOB.

As a business owner myself, I have to say that Florida is looking mighty fine with groups like FAVOB helping it every day.

DOING GOOD IS
GOOD BUSINESS

AN INTERVIEW WITH EMMA TOOPS

How an Unexpected Military Early Retirement Led to a Business That Uses a Jigsaw Puzzle Analogy to Manage Transition Chaos

Chris O'Byrne

Hi, Emma. What's a story from your childhood that you feel was instrumental in developing you into who you are today?

Emma Toops

I have two short stories from my childhood with similar themes about dinner. The first is from when I was around four years old. My parents attended an evening event, so my siblings and I had dinner with the neighbors. My parents were Filipino immigrants, and this was our first dinner with an American family.

I remember sitting at the table watching the mom set the silverware and the two little girls who were around the same age as my sister and me helping with two boxes of milk, one whole and one 2 percent. The boxes confused me since we only drank whole milk at home, and it came in a gallon jug, not a box.

When they passed the food around, which included bread

and potatoes, I was surprised that there was no rice. And when it came time to start eating, I didn't know what to do because my silverware was a knife and fork, but no spoon.

All of my expectations were based on my Filipino upbringing and usual routines. I was used to having rice at every meal, ate with a fork and spoon, and drank only whole milk. Because of my confusion, I had to watch the others eat first to figure out how to eat using only a fork.

The following story is from when I was around ten years old. My dad, who did most of the cooking, made something ethnic, possibly Filipino, for dinner, and as it was unfamiliar to me, I asked him what it was. He responded, "It's your dinner." This wasn't the response I was expecting, so I persisted and asked again, "But what *is* it?" He responded again with, "It's your dinner."

He understood his response was not what I was looking for, so he turned it into a teaching moment. He said to me, "I do the cooking around here. Do you trust me, your dad, to cook something for you that tastes good and is good for you? If so, then you know what this is? It's your dinner."

_____

"It's your dinner."
_____

That stopped any further inquiry, and I ate it regardless of my not knowing exactly what it was.

These childhood experiences highlight the diversity in people's expectations in specific environments and some ways we can learn.

When you are confused or have unmet expectations in a particular situation, something is missing either in yourself or how you show up to environmental expectations. Learning can occur through various means: observation, being told something, research, education, or through trust in others.

My work is focused on the transition process, which always involves a measure of learning and elements of environmental contexts. What people know, expect, and value in their beliefs and worldviews are based on their experience, which drives their behaviors.

_____

"The transition process always involves a measure of learning and elements of environmental contexts."
_____

I help resolve confusion or unmet expectations by helping people in their thinking and approach when in a transition. This way of thinking I teach is called the Transition Puzzle Paradigm. The specific ways I help them through their transition are based on the context they provide of themselves and their environment.

Chris O'Byrne

That's a great application of those stories. When did you decide to join the military, considering your experiences growing up and attending school?

Emma Toops

My parents, born, raised, and college-educated in the Philippines, didn't know each other when they immigrated to the US to seek better career opportunities and help support their family back in the Philippines. Mom was a neonatal RN and Dad was a machinist at John Deere Harvester, so we were a middle-income family.

My siblings and I grew up with the values of good character, support to and for the family, education, and working hard. Although our parents didn't explicitly tell us to go to college, it was ingrained in us from a young age. We were chronologically only one year apart from our next older sibling, so as a middle-income family, how can we send three students to college almost simultaneously? Mom and Dad encouraged us to pursue academic scholarships because we were smart and in the top 10% of our classes. They were unsure of other options since they had gone to college in the Philippines.

While I was athletic, I was not skilled enough to merit an athletic scholarship. Similarly, my sister and I had musical talent but were not at a level likely to earn a performance scholarship. The military was an alternative option that emerged through recruiters, guidance counselors, and other materials.

My older brother joined the National Guard after finishing one semester of his senior year and graduating early. This allowed him to fulfill military initial entry requirements of basic and advanced individual training to earn education benefits, and he started college at a state university the following fall.

I was a junior during this time, and in exploring scholarship opportunities, I learned about the Air Force ROTC scholarship, which I applied for in the spring. I later learned about the Army ROTC scholarship that summer, and I applied when I was in the first semester of my senior year.

Ultimately, I received scholarship offers from both military branches.

Chris O'Byrne

When did you enter the military? Was it immediately after graduating high school?

Emma Toops

After applying in the spring, I was offered an Air Force scholarship in the fall. However, I decided to wait before responding because

I had also applied for the Army scholarship. I wanted to see if the Army would offer a scholarship, and then I would choose.

ROTC Scholarships are awarded based on merit and program selection. The Air Force offer was a two-year scholarship focused on nursing. I, however, wanted to become a doctor and intended to be pre-med with a biology degree. On the other hand, the Army offered a three-year advanced designee scholarship in a physical science (that I could choose).

The advanced designee meant I wasn't obligated to a service commitment during my first year of college because none of my tuition was covered yet. It was like a "try it before you buy it" period. I had to meet specific academic requirements for my major and ROTC courses for the scholarship to pay tuition for the remaining three years. Alternatively, I could discontinue ROTC after the first year with no financial or service obligation.

In my mind, I wanted significant help with educational expenses, a pre-med biology degree, and a military service obligation that didn't commit me for life.

My dad, one of the most practical people I know, suggested the Air Force was more technical and focused on sophisticated equipment. In contrast, the Army, though also technical and

sophisticated, had many more people. I wanted to help as many people as possible as a medical doctor, so I accepted the Army scholarship with my seventeen-year-old naivety, logical thinking, and Dad's pragmatic advice.

I was an ROTC contracted cadet because I was going to school on a scholarship. I had an obligation to serve after I finished my degree because of the scholarship.

Chris O'Byrne

How long were you in the Army altogether?

Emma Toops

Seventeen and a half years and some change.

My original intent was to help my family pay for college and become a medical doctor; however, I changed my mind in my junior year about attending medical school. I graduated with a biology degree and entered the Army as an active-duty (full-time) commissioned officer. The ROTC scholarship obligated me to serve eight years, whether part-time in the National Guard or Army Reserve or full-time in the Regular Army. I stayed on active duty well past the obligated eight years because I enjoyed the Army and believed in my work as a Chemical Officer.

I had great success as a young Chemical Officer and eventually decided on a new objective: retire as a Lieutenant Colonel after twenty years. Unfortunately, that goal went unrealized due to a military downsize from 2010 to 2016, wherein I was expecting to get selected for promotion but lacked opportunities in the Chemical branch.

Every problem that personally involves us has our mindset or self-identity as part of our response or approach in dealing with it; however, often, there are environmental considerations that get discounted, overlooked, or are unknown.

Self and Space-Awareness is the strategic component of the Transition Puzzle Paradigm that allows us to identify and assess what we can and cannot control. There is transition chaos in the middle elements of Personal Identity, Purpose, Rules and Culture, and Routines and Expectation. It is in the middle where life happens as we manage ourselves and how we show up in a specific environment, but we can get stuck.

The lack of environmental awareness during a military drawdown contributed to my unpreparedness in my career, which ended prematurely in 2013 versus my intended retirement in 2016 or later. Now, I help people navigate transitions by teaching this paradigm to get

The Transition Puzzle Paradigm

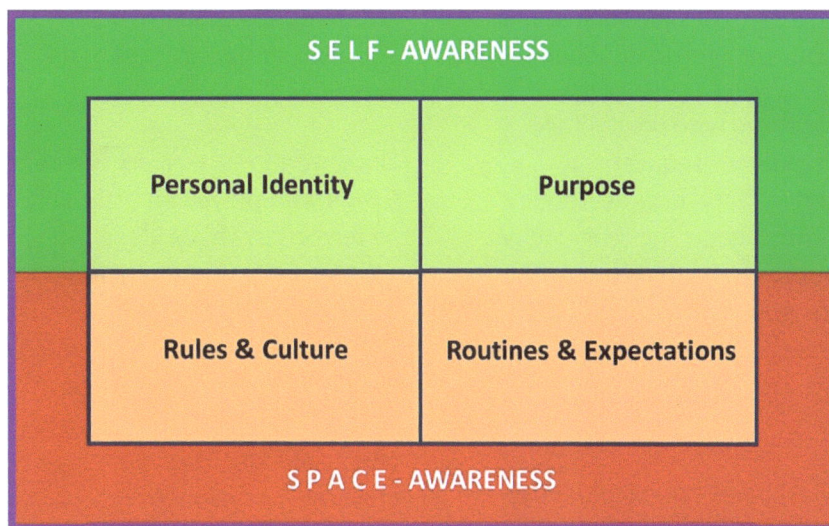

self and space-aware. Then, as they clarify the middle, they gain confidence and become more intentional in pursuing a goal because they realize what they can and cannot control.

Chris O'Byrne

After leaving the military, what made you decide to become an entrepreneur?

Emma Toops

I learned in late June 2013 that my career was ending on November 30, 2013, due to the military drawdown, whether I liked it or not. At the time, I was assigned overseas in Germany to a unit that was deactivating. I had to get reassigned to a new unit for administrative purposes, submit a request for early retirement, wait for the request to get approved, and then

work through all personal and professional transition planning concerns as quickly as possible. After out-processing the unit, I was on leave for my last ninety days of active duty and returned to the US in September 2013.

"I learned in late June 2013 that my career was ending on November 30, 2013, due to the military drawdown, whether I liked it or not."

Initially, I intended to pursue career opportunities in government agencies such as Homeland Security, Federal Emergency Management Agency (FEMA), Environmental Protection Agency (EPA), or the Center for Disease Control (CDC), agencies where my military experience was most relevant. Unfortunately, the government shut down under sequestration in October.

I realized with the military drawdown, sequestration, and military and government contracts getting canceled or not renewed that working for the government was not a wise choice, especially since I had very little time before my military career ended.

Most people don't understand what I did in the military, so let me explain briefly.

As a Chemical Officer, my subject matter technical expertise was in identifying and mitigating unconventional risks associated with chemical, biological, radiation, and nuclear (CBRN) threats. I also had soft skills in leadership, communication, planning, operations, organizational development, and organizational management.

Conventional military risks are visible loud, create explosions, or penetrate objects such as bullets, rockets, and cannons. Their destructive capabilities are obvious, and you can see them coming. Unconventional risks, however, are invisible, not necessarily a projectile, or not used primarily for destructive purposes. Exposure to CBRN can also be innocuous in that it exists naturally in the environment (germs, viruses, the sun) or through accidents (vehicle or facility mishaps) but can potentially cause harm merely because of unawareness of its presence.

Unconventional warfare is when CBRN is employed intentionally by terrorists. This is illegal, unexpected, unpredictable, and unusual. The effects of unconventional warfare are often catastrophic or chaotic in emotional and physical harm to people at a small scale (biological, chemical, or radioactive dirty bomb) and a weapon of mass destruction when used on a large scale (intercontinental ballistic missiles). Regardless, exposure to CBRN risks can incapacitate people nearly as much in fear as in its physical effects.

Mitigating CBRN risks is primarily in understanding potential risk exposure, the consequences to people if they are not informed or protected, the consequences to the planned operation if communication or mobility is compromised by protective gear or the exposure risk, and offering guidance for mission planning and execution when or if CBRN is encountered or employed to achieve outcomes that more closely resemble expectations.

So, in understanding how my general skills and experience might translate to a non-military environment, I decided to pursue an entrepreneurial opportunity in insurance or financial advising. These occupations are similarly about risk identification, risk mitigation, consultative communication, and guidance, often about complicated or uncomfortable topics that lead to decisions that pursue a goal.

Whether I entered the private sector, pursued entrepreneurship, or took any other path, all of them would be challenging because I didn't know anyone outside the military. The military people I knew were scattered across different locations. And if they were no longer in the military, I had no idea what they were doing. Therefore, I saw entrepreneurship as a less risky option for applying myself in a new environment, and I planned to pursue an opportunity that already had a proven business model.

Once I decided on the financial services industry as my objective, I researched opportunities and talked to people with industry experience. When starting out, one of my husband's friends, who had been a financial advisor for over fifteen years, suggested aligning myself with big brands like Farmers or Edwards Jones. These were well-recognized and would help me quickly build credibility since I did not yet have a brand or reputation in business.

I started a from-scratch insurance agency, Emma Toops' Agency:

Farmers Insurance, in January 2014, after spending my first month studying for and testing for my Property and Casualty, Life, and Health insurance licenses. I was a 1099 contractor with Farmers Insurance and built my business for almost a year. In meeting many new people over ten months in networking groups, community engagement activities, and through referrals, I learned a lot about business culture, processes, language, and the like, but I also observed a perpetual gap of understanding for military culture between me and non-military people.

Inevitably, when I met someone new, my transition story would come up for how I was in insurance after being in the military. Depending on the person, their familiarity with my military background or my familiarity with their business varied. I realized over time that whenever there was confusion on their part or mine, I was bridging the understanding gap.

> **"I realized over time that whenever there was confusion on their part or mine, I was bridging the understanding gap."**

What I observed in my interactions that were different than many people in similar situations is that when a gap existed and I was the one confused, I'd ask questions to clear up my confusion, transparently admitting my incompetence on the topic at hand. On the flip side, if the confusion was about military culture, jargon, or behavior, I often picked up on their confusion and explained it. I realized that many people are unwilling to reveal their ignorance and ask a question or don't want to be bothered by explaining complicated or serious topics.

My military background was very educational and consultative on urgent or serious issues, so I find explaining and educating very comfortable and easy. I do it often, as it is one of my realized strengths.

It was this realization that education was the key to bridging the gap that I later launched my current company, Toops Consulting, with my husband, David. However, to understand how that pivot came about, I need to explain part of David's transition story.

In my time in the military, David was the military spouse, and I was the active-duty service member. His technical expertise is in computer science, specifically computer programming and databases. Unfortunately, his programmer and software developer work was sporadic as it depended on our location and available opportunities.

There were times when he was voluntarily unemployed and taking care of family with medical concerns versus taking employment well below his abilities. There were also times when he did volunteer work to support my career, such as the Family Readiness Group Leader when I was in command or volunteering with the brigade or installation for family or community support.

When I retired and started building an insurance agency, David worked for a high school friend, briefly doing project management and operations work. After that, he found it very difficult to find employment that applied his computer and information technology skills, even though he has two master's degrees and was working with a technical recruiter. The problem was primarily because he didn't know anyone and wasn't well understood in the traditional hiring process. His resume had gaps in employment, his expertise wasn't inherently apparent for the paid work he did have while I was serving, and his being a military spouse was certainly not well understood.

What happened to bring us to start our own company was something David said in a conversation when I asked how things were going with the technical recruiter.

Long story short, he was not getting pitched as an ideal candidate for various opportunities due to changes in some of the computer languages over time where, due to errors in syntax in some skills tests, his code wasn't at the level of proficiency that the employers demanded, which was set unusually high at 90 percent. I thought this odd since certification requirements usually pass at 70 percent, and David scored in the 85–87 percentile.

What was especially frustrating for him is that computer programming is like understanding a foreign language. And just like regular spoken languages, once you are fluent in them, loss of fluency is because of lack of regular usage. However, fluency is quickly regained when exposed to it regularly. Any changes in the language are quickly learned, just like when spoken vocabulary

changes over time, but he wasn't getting opportunities to be around the language regularly to regain fluency.

"My response to him was, 'Why don't we?'"

He said in utter frustration, "If I have to explain myself to everyone I meet to be found credible because of gaps in my resume or they don't understand me because of superficial reasons, then I should just be a consultant and work for myself!" My response to him was, "Why don't we?"

He was initially confused by my response since what he said was in exasperation, but I explained to him my realization of the military and non-military understanding gap, and it was education that bridged it. I suggested that we both had relevant technical expertise to offer as consultants, and we also happened to be good at explaining and educating people on simple or more complicated topics. We both had tutored peers in high school and college, went to college with wrestling and ROTC scholarships, had experience teaching teens or adults, my military career had been primarily in training and education, and I had a Master of Education: Curriculum and Instruction. So, we discussed how we might leverage our experience to create a business in the knowledge industry.

I informed my district manager at Farmers about the idea of me pivoting from my insurance agency, and he supported it, even mentioning a Farmers marketing campaign focused on attracting military talent. He emphasized that people are willing to pay for expertise and efficiency. So, I wound down operations for my insurance agency in about a month, and David and I started Toops Consulting, LLC in December 2014.

"People are willing to pay for expertise and efficiency."

Chris O'Byrne

What makes Toops Consulting unique?

Emma Toops

Confidence in your abilities to meet expectations and believing in the value of what you can deliver is crucial when starting a knowledge-based start-up, even if you're initially unknown.

David and I knew no one in Kansas City when we moved here, and I chose to become an entrepreneur as the first thing out of the gates when I retired from the Army. Our experience was not in business, but our technical and soft skills were transferable to a new industry or business environment. We didn't know a lot, but we were willing to learn.

We were applying the principles of the Transition Puzzle Paradigm. I realized it later in self-reflection when I wondered how we could do what we did, considering our circumstances, and not have it be an epic failure.

Our business, Toops Consulting, was initially designed with three business segments: 1) Personal and Professional Development, 2) IT Consulting, and 3) Military Programs and Strategies. We both offer expertise in personal and professional development; David is the IT consultant, and I provide expertise in Military Programs and Strategies.

We learned over time, however, that marketing three separate business segments was challenging to do effectively without confusing people about our specific offers.

We also connected to more personal and professional development opportunities since education and personal growth are commonly relatable and understood. People in the market always seek education, expertise, and ways to accelerate processes that achieve objectives.

Our marketing focuses on personal and professional development that supports students and adults in academic or career transitions. We offer the Strengths Profile assessment, contract teaching, subject tutoring, ACT Exam Prep, academic coaching, career development planning, and networking strategies in this niche.

> *"Our marketing is specifically on personal and professional development that supports students and adults in academic or career transitions."*

We have a unique affinity to the military transitioner, and we are active in the non-profit and military-support community and offer transition support services. We are also open to consulting projects, but opportunities are provided primarily through referrals.

Chris O'Byrne

Switching gears a little, who were some key influences or mentors who helped you get where you are now?

Emma Toops

As a second lieutenant, I was introduced to John C. Maxwell's book, *The 21 Irrefutable Laws of Leadership*, an excellent tool for understanding leadership early on in my career. One concept that has stuck with me over the decades is leadership is influence, and anyone can possess it.

After leaving the military, I discovered Napoleon Hill's *Think and Grow Rich*, which introduced me to thirteen success principles, specifically the concepts of infinite intelligence and masterminds. These ideas expanded my perspectives on the power to achieve whatever you desire, which lies in accessing universal energy and knowledge through a collective effort with others.

I also like Dean Graziosi, who wrote *Millionaire Success Habits* and *The Underdog Advantage*. A few of his teachings that resonate with me are turning your mess into your message and the advantage of being an underdog. He asserts that when you've overcome messes in life, you gain expertise and insight to help others who are not yet where you are in that experience. And when you are deemed an underdog, people have no or low expectations for what you are capable of, which allows you anonymity and much less pressure for outcomes. Then, when you demonstrate capabilities or show results that are well above those low expectations, you surprise everyone and are a rock star.

These three business authors have influenced how I conduct myself and my business through guidance I've encountered in their books, but I've also had individuals who have personally coached or mentored me to accelerate my entrepreneurial growth.

Ultimately, the Transition Puzzle Paradigm is how I think, where self and spatial awareness create the framework for managing the chaotic middle, where life and transitions occur.

The paradigm emphasizes acknowledging and understanding what you can and cannot control. Take control of what you can and learn to influence the rest. With clarity comes confidence, drive, and action.

"With clarity comes confidence, drive, and action."

The more clarity you have for personal identity, purpose, rules and culture, and routines and expectations, the more intentional you are in actions because there are fewer unknowns. Self-confidence paired with purpose generates unlimited energy that allows you to overcome barriers, even if there is much to learn or you lack the necessary resources. You become resourceful and seek out the things and people you need to accelerate your progress.

Chris O'Byrne

Reflecting on your entrepreneurial journey, what is one of your most valuable lessons?

Emma Toops

If you can, apply yourself to your strengths! Your performance, energy, and drive will be higher when you do, which results in greater outcomes for you and your business.

As a Strengths Profile practitioner, I strive to help others understand their strengths, learned behaviors, and weaknesses. This self-awareness is valuable for intentional decisions in how you show up to others and your actions.

Also, be curious and innovative for continuous improvement in your systems and processes, creating new relationships, or exploring new markets.

You never know when or if a chance encounter with someone sparks a big idea or revelation that becomes a new product, service, pivot, or partner opportunity.

Being objective, confident, and open to continuous learning is crucial to avoid getting stuck. Be receptive to new ideas and perspectives, whether you are a beginner or an expert. By embracing a lifelong learner mindset, you can overcome any challenge.

REALIZED STRENGTHS		
Strengths you use and enjoy		
Perform Well	Energizing	Higher Use
Use Wisely		

UNREALIZED STRENGTHS		
Strengths you don't use as often		
Perform Well	Energizing	Lower Use
Use More		

LEARNED BEHAVIORS		
Things you've learned to do but may not enjoy		
Perform Well	De-Energizing	Variable Use
Use When Needed		

WEAKNESSES		
Things you find hard and don't enjoy		
Perform Poorly	De-Energizing	Variable Use
Use Less		

Self and space awareness are the framework for your focus, so be as clear as you can with it to manage the transition chaos of the middle more effectively.

You don't have to do everything yourself, and it's common for individuals to hinder their progress by thinking otherwise. The half of the puzzle you control is yourself – get help from others for the other half.

Chris O'Byrne

What is the best way for people to learn more about you and your work?

Emma Toops

I am on LinkedIn at www.linkedin.com/in/emmatoops. Additionally, visit my website at www.toopsconsulting.com to learn how we help students, adults, and the military transitioner with coaching, or businesses for public speaking and organizational development.

Schedule an appointment or discovery call at www.toopsconsulting.as.me or email me at emma@toopsconsulting.com.

About the Author

An ROTC Distinguished Military Graduate and Army Veteran with 17.5 years of active-duty experience.

Emma is a retired Army Major who served in the US, South Korea, and Germany; had two company commands; and deployed to Iraq and Afghanistan.

Emma's military expertise with training, education, environmental risk identification and mitigation, and organizational leadership led her to entrepreneurship and community service after retiring from the Army in 2013.

NAVIGATING THE CRYPTO FRONTIER: A DEEP DIVE WITH CHARLIE STIVERS

Chris O'Byrne

Charlie, thank you for joining the show. I'm thrilled to have you here to discuss your work in the crypto industry. I came across your profile through *GOO$E Magazine*, and I'd love for you to share more about that connection. Additionally, I'm curious to learn about your other ventures and interests.

Charlie Stivers

Sure! I started my journey in the tech field, pursuing a career in tech during my schooling years. Unfortunately, I lost my father, and as one of seven kids, we had life insurance. Growing up, my father guided us to invest $25 monthly in mutual funds. When I received a small amount of life insurance, I didn't want to squander it like many people

do. Being passionate about technology and the dotcom boom in the late '90s, I invested in several dotcom companies and experienced significant success. It was a favorable time for such investments. In 2001, I pursued my interest further and obtained my financial planning license. This led to a seventeen-year career in the field, during which I wrote a book called *The Social Security Success Guide*, focusing on retirement income strategies and social security. I thoroughly enjoyed my career, especially engaging in seminar marketing, conducting classes, and public speaking.

After a bad mishap in cannabis investing, I learned a valuable lesson about what not to do in investing. During the lockdowns in March 2020, I became interested in Bitcoin and Ethereum. With extra time, I delved deeply into researching blockchain technology and its potential impact on the future. I concluded that it is essentially the evolution of the internet. This led me to purchase my first Bitcoin and Ethereum, and it opened a whole new world of crypto and blockchain.

From my finance background, I learned the importance of reading *Rich Dad, Poor Dad* by Robert Kiyosaki. He emphasizes that the wealthy invest in income-producing assets. Applying this concept to the world of crypto, I explored passive income strategies like yield farming and decentralized finance. These methods bypass intermediaries, which worries the government and banks. By leveraging existing financial models, we can generate significant profits.

We've previously talked about leadership, and now we're exploring professionalism in cryptocurrency development, particularly in decentralized finance and data transmission over the blockchain. It's incredibly intriguing to see how data is being hailed as the new oil, which aligns with the idea that blockchain is the next step in the evolution of the internet. I believe this is the direction everything is heading, and I'm excited to be involved and support others in this journey.

Chris O'Byrne

I have all sorts of questions that I want to ask, but one of my first questions—and I've been investing in crypto for a while—is, when will crypto become mainstream?

Charlie Stivers

That's the golden question, for sure. The mainstream adoption of crypto will likely happen incrementally. For instance, PayPal recently introduced stablecoins, which are tied to the value of the US dollar. This allows for easier payment for goods and services. PayPal is already a major payment provider, ranking third in the industry. Additionally, Visa, the largest payment provider, has announced a partnership with Solana, which will be interesting to observe.

I'm interested in exploring why they chose Solana. However, the true adoption of crypto by the masses will come from its utility in everyday transactions, such as micropayments for goods and services. Currently, crypto remains niche-oriented.

Secondly, is institutional adoption. Exchange Traded Funds, or ETFs, will facilitate large injections of liquidity in Bitcoin and Ethereum driving prices up which will attract attention to crypto markets again. In fact, the Department of Defense is utilizing blockchain technology for secure data transmission, as highlighted in the magazine's first issue. While the Department of Defense is progressing, our legislators are still debating regulations for crypto, causing delays and disagreements. This is driving jobs and capital abroad and we may see mass adoptions in other countries first.

Chris O'Byrne

There's a lot to unpack in that question. Let's focus on decentralized finance. Where are things with that? Will it become a reality, or will it be a challenging journey?

Charlie Stivers

Decentralized financing has various models, including decentralized exchanges, which lack oversight and regulations. Leadership and criteria development are crucial for success. Government concerns arise due to potential impacts on banks, which have significant global influence.

Therefore, it's super disruptive, allowing for the elimination of intermediaries and generating significant profits. However, the US may face challenges due to regulatory frameworks. The evolution of decentralized finance will likely consider the interests of banks. It's important to note that decentralized finance is just a small component of the broader financial landscape.

Decentralized finance is expected to be highly disruptive, comparable to how email affected the US Postal Service. This disruption could potentially cause a crash or have other significant effects. Bitcoin has already served as a safe-haven during times of bank failures. However, cryptocurrency has also been scapegoated during such incidents, as seen in the case of FTX and Silicon Valley Bank.

The credit crisis and bank crash in 2007–2008 exposed the fragility of the banking system. Bitcoin was born out of this crisis, and the readers may be familiar with fractionalized banking. During that time, banks were leveraging their deposits at a ratio of fourteen to seventeen times, which was later reduced to about ten times. Banks still leverage and lend out assets up to ten times the amount on their balance sheet.

In the movie *It's a Wonderful Life* with George Bailey, there were runs on banks, but not as common as today, where you can withdraw funds with a simple click. If many depositors want to withdraw their money digitally simultaneously, banks may not have enough capital to meet the demand, as we have witnessed in the past.

Chris O'Byrne

How would decentralized finance specifically benefit the average person? It eliminates the need for banks and has minimum requirements, but how does that directly impact regular individuals?

Charlie Stivers

In a decentralized model, you have wallets on your phone, browser extension, or external (cold) device. The wallets are encrypted with a twelve-word passphrase. It's important to treat this twelve-word passphrase like gold and protect it. If you get a new device, you can install the wallet on it. However, be cautious, as others with access to the passphrase can do the same.

Decentralization means true ownership with self-custody of coins and tokens. In the future, we will likely have custody over digital dollars as well. Wallets are encoded, eliminating the need for passwords and logins. Connecting a wallet gives you access to a platform for depositing money. By pledging assets, you can earn yield with varying risk tolerance levels. Higher APY means higher risk, while lower risk corresponds to lower APY. Think in terms of a CDs versus bonds.

Decentralized protocols on the blockchain are transparent and verified by third-party audit companies. They eliminate the need for middlemen and allow for quick withdrawal of funds.

Decentralized finance allows retail borrowers to easily pledge their assets and obtain a loan without needing an underwriter or selling assets.

Chris O'Byrne

Explain micropayments a little more.

Charlie Stivers

Micropayments are super fascinating. Bitcoin is already using the Lightning Network to achieve this. In the first edition of *GOO$E*, I wrote a story called "The Rise of the Young Bitcoin User," which covered this topic. Seeing how the school found a sponsor to support the students' entrepreneurial endeavors was fascinating. They gave each interested student $50 to start their own small businesses and showcased them at a little business fair, like a science fair in the gymnasium. Some of my friends heard about this and got involved as well.

We raised funds through the Rocky Mountain Bitcoiners, collecting about $500 in Bitcoin.

We used the user-friendly Muun wallet and taught the kids how to install and secure it. Each student received $5 and went shopping at their friends' businesses.

It's a $5 Bitcoin transaction on the Lightning Network with a fee of just 4 cents, less than 1 percent. It's immediate, hit receive and invoice, scan the QR code, hit invoice, and the payment settles instantly into your account. With such a low transaction fee, it's easy to ask restaurant servers if they want to be tipped in Bitcoin, generating conversation. Some vendors at the POS register are also starting to accept crypto payments.

Here's a business tip: Consider adding Bitcoin as a payment method to your small business website or brick-and-mortar store. Bitcoiners in your city actively seek out businesses that accept Bitcoin as a way to spend their digital currency.

Chris O'Byrne

For somebody like me who has an online store, in a sense—an online business—what's the easiest way to start accepting Bitcoin?

Charlie Stivers

One simple way to start accepting Bitcoin for your brick-and-mortar business is through a partnership with Strike and Clover. Strike is a payment platform that allows customers

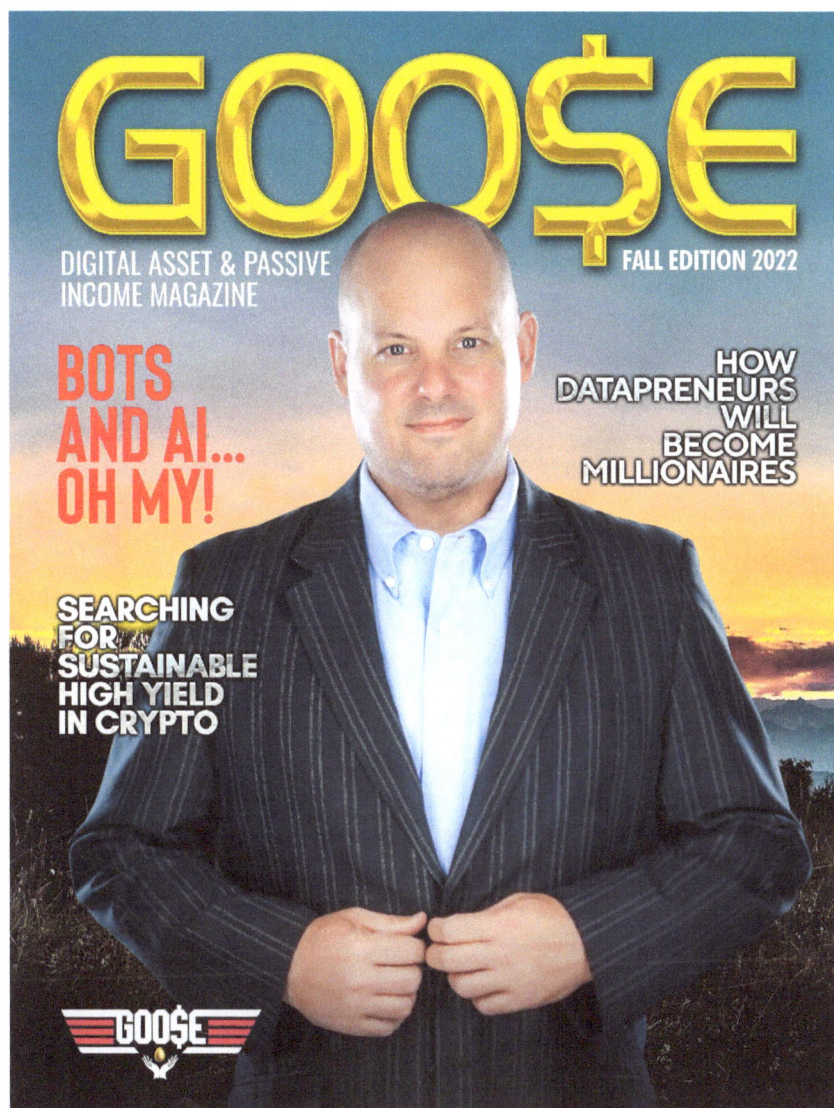

to pay in Bitcoin, and Clover is a popular point-of-sale system. By integrating Strike with Clover, you can offer your customers Bitcoin as a payment option.

With Strike, you have the flexibility to choose how much of the payment you want to keep in Bitcoin and how much you want to convert to cash. For example, you can set it up to keep 50 percent in Bitcoin and 50 percent in cash, which will be deposited

into your bank account. This allows you to benefit from Bitcoin's potential growth while still having most of your funds readily available for day-to-day operations.

As a Bitcoin believer, it can be wise to keep some Bitcoin on the side, especially in the early stages when a small percentage of your customers may choose to pay with Bitcoin. By diversifying your business capital and adding

Bitcoin to your balance sheet, you can potentially benefit from the long-term growth of cryptocurrency.

Chris O'Byrne

Currently, if I want to get paid, I send somebody an invoice through my accounting program. What would be the difference then if I wanted to get paid through Bitcoin? How would I send that?

Charlie Stivers

Typically, a QR code is used for this purpose. It's simple—just scan the QR code to generate the wallet address or copy and paste the wallet address. This will become easier with experience.

Chris O'Byrne

Is that done through the software they have on their phone?

Charlie Stivers

There are various options available, including mobile apps. Wallets can provide this function, while I can't recall a specific brand for online invoices now, a few emerging ones will be available soon.

Chris O'Byrne

Got it. If someone wants to send an invoice through PayPal, they can currently choose to pay using PayPal or a credit card. Additionally, PayPal's investment in their Stablecoin may introduce another option in the future.

Charlie Stivers

In the future, you'll also have the option to screenshot the QR code or email or direct message it to someone. If they can scan it with their wallet, they can instantly pay.

Chris O'Byrne

So, it's still not the easiest for people in a sense, but it's not that complicated either. It just takes a little education.

Charlie Stivers

Yeah, there are ways to shorten the process. Those who are familiar with Bitcoin and crypto do it regularly. I have already done it myself. That's one of the advantages of being in the crypto industry. We can simply copy and paste the wallet address and send it, which functions similarly. The

key is to ensure that you copy and paste the address accurately. It becomes routine once you've mastered it, just like any other technology. However, what you're referring to is more like a professional invoicing system that offers customers different payment options. I haven't come across a professional solution for that yet.

Chris O'Byrne

That's what I was wondering because I know many people would be like, "Yeah, I'm more than willing to accept Bitcoin, but I want to make it super easy and incorporate it into what I'm already doing."

Charlie Stivers

That day is coming.

Chris O'Byrne

I'm excited about that. I'm a crypto believer. I think it's almost all but inevitable how it will take over and change our lives.

Charlie Stivers

Regarding other things I do, I have a CBD and hemp marketplace website where I accept coin-based payments. Some people have already paid with cryptocurrency through this platform. While bigger ecommerce companies have solutions for this, finding an invoicing system for small business owners like us may not be as readily available. Such a system may exist, but I don't know of one off the top of my head.

Chris O'Byrne

Blockchain is not just limited to cryptocurrency; it has various applications. For instance, I've been exploring blockchain in relation to copyright for books. There's a concept called blockchain copyright, which can be interesting for authors. I've also explored NFTs for book covers and ebook interiors. These are just a few examples of how blockchain and NFTs can be utilized by businesspeople. Can you think of any other potential applications in this context?

Charlie Stivers

To begin, let's define blockchain or distributed ledger technology (DLT). Blockchain is essentially a public ledger of debits and credits that all users can witness. It offers a level of anonymity, but it's not 100 percent private. Initially, it was primarily used as a payment method on the dark web.

Technology now enables regulators, governments, and the IRS to trace the origin of funds in blockchain transactions. This has led to increased regulations, including anti-money laundering measures. Even decentralized entities are being required to comply with these regulations. The aim is for custodians to

be responsible for monitoring transactions, although authorities can still track users regardless.

Blockchain is a public platform that provides proof of ownership. For example, as the creator of a book, you can create and sell NFTs digitally and have digital and print variations of that same book. This gives you control over your creations.

In the case of a popular or limited book, you can now sell the rights or ownership on a secondary market using blockchain. The blockchain traces the ownership back to the creator, like how artists benefit from NFTs in the art world. The creator receives residual payments every time the book is sold on the secondary market. This concept can be applied to proof of ownership in various fields, such as vehicles, homes, and intellectual property, adding value to the owner. NFTs or crypto tokens can be used to sell fractions or portions of these assets.

That's what's driving the value of blockchain. People often wonder what gives blockchain or crypto its value. It's not just the utility but primarily the large network of users. This is creating a vast marketplace for free market business, with each country having its own regulations. However, the goal is to create a decentralized community of individuals who want to engage

in business, travel, and spend money across borders. While this is the ideal scenario, there are also individuals who disrupt this harmony, leading to the need for regulations and laws.

Chris O'Byrne

What are some innovative uses you've seen for smart contracts?

Charlie Stivers

An example of an innovative use for smart contracts is ticketing for events. Currently, third-party brokers profit heavily from ticket fees. With smart contracts, producers and artists can sell tickets directly to consumers, regardless of the event's scale. Each ticket is assigned a unique QR code recorded on the blockchain. Attendees can simply show their phones at the event entrance, like existing QR-code-based ticketing systems. However, the key difference is that the transaction is recorded on the blockchain, ensuring that the smart contract executes exactly as intended. Smart contracts are essentially unchangeable software on the blockchain designed to perform specific functions. Creators will love this solution because they can get royalties even if it is sold on the secondary market, cutting out ticket brokers.

Another use case for NFTs could be a pizza shop selling a $50 NFT with attractive branding. This offers commercial advantages and adds value to the artwork, making it a collectible item. This serves as a small business example of the potential of NFTs for branding and profitability.

Anyone with the NFT can use it to get discounts by showing it in person or scanning the QR code online. There can be different levels of discounts, like 25 percent off for early adopters who spend over $20, limited to 100 people. There can also be a second series with fewer benefits, also limited to 100 people. NFTs reward creativity and offer unique opportunities to build a loyal customer base and encourage repeat business. The possibilities for NFTs are vast and exciting.

Chris O'Byrne

I've been fascinated by the connection between cryptocurrency and books for a while. I've invested in two companies related to ebook platforms, even though they haven't gained much traction yet. I still believe in their potential and want to see them succeed. How would I do that if I wanted to create an NFT from an ebook or book cover? How does one go about creating an NFT?

Charlie Stivers

Typically, if you have a design team for your cover, they just need to use a specific file format. Some marketplaces facilitate the creation of NFTs.

Once you're in the decentralized marketplace, converting your design into an NFT is fairly straightforward. Different file formats are accepted. From there, you can decide on your strategy, whether it's creating a collection, limited editions, or one-of-a-kind pieces. This strategic decision impacts the rarity, value, and collectability of the NFT. It will be interesting to see how this creator marketplace empowers creators to be properly compensated for their work.

We've seen this phenomenon with artists who captivate us with their cool profile pictures. Some limited collections, like *Vee Friends* by Gary Vaynerchuk, have gained significant traction due to the artist's large following. The scarcity of these NFTs, with only 10,000 available, creates a high demand. This has also led to the onboarding of many new users into the NFT space.

In some cases, it's helpful for us followers to learn and grow our businesses. He showed people how to onboard, and those who did made a ton of money. However, just like most of the other NFT collections, the value has decreased, but he has a lot of benefits behind his collection, which drives its value. As a creator and developer, the belief in your ability to grow the community adds additional value to the secondary market. The incentive of royalties is built in for you to build that community.

And then you're generating revenue. It's a business. You can pay staff; you can pay your good creators. If you manage your money like a business, you can grow that into a very profitable endeavor.

Chris O'Byrne

It's almost unlimited, all the possibilities, which is just part of

what fascinates me with it. So, what's a common platform for creating an NFT?

Charlie Stivers

OpenSea.io was once the largest NFT marketplace but now faces competition from various platforms, including those on different blockchains like Solana. Bitcoin has also entered the NFT space with its own protocol and projects like Ordinals. These developments show the potential for scalability and innovation in the NFT ecosystem. As developers continue to improve existing technology and build applications on different layers of blockchains, the possibilities for growth and advancement are limitless.

Chris O'Byrne

Great. And that's what drove me to invest in Solana in the first place, looking into the NFTs and exploring that. We could be talking about so much more, but I think we need to wrap it up for this episode. There'll be more. Where is the best place for people to learn more about you?

Charlie Stivers

We are focused on building goosemag.com as a crypto-friendly media company, publishing in print and digital formats. Our website serves as a valuable resource and a way to get in touch with us.

Chris O'Byrne

Thank you for joining me and discussing these fascinating topics. The possibilities in the crypto world are vast and exciting, and the future is uncertain but full of potential. I look forward to seeing where it all leads.

Charlie Stivers

I encourage people to start learning and position themselves for the next bull run in the crypto market. While it's still an experiment, I believe that just like the dotcom era, we will see many of these big crypto players emerge as technology leaders. It's an exciting time to be involved in this space.

Action Steps

1. **Explore smart contracts for your business:** The author outlines how smart contracts can be used to bypass third-party brokers, especially in ticketing for events. Investigate how implementing smart contracts could reduce costs and increase efficiency in your own business operations.

2. **Create NFTs for branding and customer loyalty:** The article discusses using NFTs to build a loyal customer base. Consider launching an

NFT collection that offers special discounts or perks to your customers.

3. **Educate yourself on crypto regulations:** The author emphasizes the increasing regulations around blockchain transactions. Keep yourself updated on these to ensure you're in compliance and can navigate the crypto space safely and effectively.

About the Author

Charlie Stivers, a business owner since 2001 with strong family farm values, began his journey from a tech enthusiast who invested in dotcom stocks in 1998 to a professional licensed in 2001. In 2016, he authored the *Social Security Success Guide* to aid retirees, and in 2020, he embraced cryptocurrencies. Now, he focuses full-time on educating others about blockchain technology and helping people improve their personal economy. His vision is to grow *GOO$E* into a community-powered publication, emphasizing sustainability and responsible leadership in the decentralized digital asset space.

HARNESSING AI TO SKYROCKET YOUR SALES: A STEP-BY-STEP GUIDE

CHRIS O'BYRNE

Artificial Intelligence (AI) is no longer a futuristic concept; it's a necessity for businesses that want to stay competitive. In the sales domain, AI offers unparalleled advantages, from automating mundane tasks to providing deep customer insights. It enables businesses to operate more efficiently, make data-driven decisions, and ultimately, increase revenue. In a landscape where customer expectations are ever-evolving and fierce competition, AI is a critical differentiator.

The objective of this article is straightforward: to equip established business owners like you with a step-by-step guide to harnessing the power of AI. We're not talking about theoretical benefits or vague concepts. Instead, you'll get actionable steps that you can implement immediately to leverage AI for tangible sales growth. Whether you're struggling with lead generation, customer segmentation, or predictive analytics, this guide will serve as a roadmap to elevate your sales strategy through AI.

Understanding AI's Role in Sales

Artificial Intelligence (AI) is the simulation of human intelligence in machines programmed to think, learn, and make decisions. In the context of sales, AI can analyze large data sets quickly and provide insights that would take a human significantly longer to identify.

Key Areas Where AI Impacts Sales

Lead Generation

AI can sift through vast amounts of data to identify potential customers more likely to convert. It can analyze online behavior, social media interactions, and other metrics to pinpoint high-quality leads.

For example, you can use AI tools to scan social media for mentions of keywords related to your product and then target those users with personalized ads.

Customer Segmentation

Traditional segmentation often relies on basic variables like age, location, or past purchases. AI takes this a step further by analyzing more complex patterns in customer behavior, allowing for highly targeted marketing.

For example, you can implement AI algorithms that segment customers based on their interaction with your website, such as the pages they visit most frequently or the products they view, to send more personalized email campaigns.

Predictive Analytics

AI can analyze past sales data to predict future customer behavior, market trends, and sales opportunities. This enables businesses to be proactive rather than reactive.

For example, you can use predictive analytics to identify which seasonal products will likely be best-sellers, allowing you to manage inventory more efficiently.

Understanding these key areas will help you identify where AI can most benefit your sales strategy, setting the stage for the actionable steps outlined in the following sections.

Preparing Your Business for AI Integration

Before diving into AI, it's crucial to understand your existing sales processes clearly. Map out your sales funnel, from lead generation to customer retention. Identify the metrics you currently track and how you measure success.

Identify Gaps and Opportunities

Once you have a comprehensive view of your sales processes, pinpoint areas where you're falling short or where there's room for improvement. Are you struggling with lead quality? Is your customer segmentation too broad? These gaps are where AI can provide the most value.

Choose the Right AI Tools

You can now select the AI tools that best suit your needs based on the gaps and opportunities you've identified. Here are some considerations:

Functionality: Does the tool address your specific gap or opportunity?

Ease of Use: Is the tool user-friendly, or is there a steep learning curve?

Integration: Can it easily integrate with your existing systems, like CRM or email marketing platforms?

Budget: Does it offer a good ROI for the cost?

Implementing AI for Lead Generation

Steps to Integrate AI into Your Lead Generation Strategy

Select the AI Tool: Choose an AI tool specialized in lead

generation, such as InsideSales.com or HubSpot's AI features.

Data Input: Ensure your existing customer and lead data is clean and organized before importing it into the AI system.

Configuration: Set up the tool according to your specific lead generation goals. This could involve defining the characteristics of a high-quality lead.

Training: Brief your sales and marketing teams on how to use the tool effectively.

Launch: First, roll out the AI tool on a small scale, monitor its performance, and make any necessary adjustments before full-scale implementation.

Monitoring and Adjusting Your Approach

Performance Metrics: Track key performance indicators (KPIs) like lead quality, conversion rates, and ROI.

Regular Reviews: Schedule weekly or bi-weekly reviews to assess the tool's performance.

Adjustments: Based on the data, adjust the AI tool's settings or your overall lead generation strategy.

Use AI Analytics to Refine Your Email Marketing Campaigns

After implementing an AI tool, you can use its analytics to refine your email marketing. For instance, the tool might identify that emails sent on Tuesdays have a higher open rate. You can then adjust your email campaigns to send more critical

communications on that day for better engagement.

Leveraging AI for Customer Segmentation

How AI Can Segment Customers More Effectively Than Traditional Methods

AI goes beyond basic demographic data to offer more nuanced customer segmentation. It can analyze various factors, including behavioral patterns, browsing history, and social media interactions, to create highly targeted customer segments. This allows for more personalized and effective marketing campaigns.

Steps to Implement

Choose the Right Tool: Opt for an AI tool specializing in customer segmentation, such as Adobe Analytics or Salesforce Einstein.

Data Preparation: As with lead generation, ensure your customer data is clean and well-organized before importing it into the AI system.

Define Objectives: Clearly outline what you aim to achieve with improved customer segmentation, such as increased engagement or higher conversion rates.

Configuration: Set up the AI tool to focus on the specific customer attributes most relevant to your objectives.

Test and Deploy: Initially, test the AI tool on a smaller customer segment to evaluate its effectiveness before rolling it out fully.

Use AI Algorithms to Segment Customers Based on Buying Behavior

Implement an AI tool that tracks customer interactions with your online store. The tool can segment customers into groups like frequent buyers, discount shoppers, or window shoppers based on their buying behavior. This allows you to tailor marketing campaigns to each segment, increasing the likelihood of conversion.

By leveraging AI for customer segmentation, you can create more targeted marketing campaigns that resonate with specific customer groups, increasing engagement and conversions.

Utilizing Predictive Analytics

Predictive analytics uses historical data and machine learning algorithms to forecast future outcomes. This can mean predicting customer behaviors, market trends, and sales revenue in sales. It lets you make proactive decisions, optimizing your sales strategy for future success.

How to Implement It in Your Sales Strategy

Select the Tool: Choose a predictive analytics tool that fits your needs, such as IBM's Watson Analytics or SAP Analytics Cloud.

Data Collection: Ensure the tool has sufficient historical sales data to analyze.

Define Objectives: Clearly state what you aim to predict, whether it's customer behavior, sales for a specific product, or overall revenue.

Model Training: Use past data to train the predictive model. This may require collaboration with data scientists or analysts.

Deployment: Once the model is trained and tested, deploy it to start making predictions.

Ongoing Monitoring: Regularly update the model with new data and adjust your sales strategies based on the predictions.

Use Predictive Analytics to Forecast Which Products Will Be Best-Sellers

After collecting past sales data, use a predictive analytics tool to identify trends in product popularity. The tool can forecast which products will likely be best-sellers in the coming months. With this information, you can adjust your inventory levels, marketing strategies, and pricing to maximize revenue.

By implementing predictive analytics into your sales strategy, you're not just reacting to the market but staying ahead. This proactive approach can give you a significant competitive edge.

Measuring ROI and Making Adjustments

Key Performance Indicators to Track

ROI: The ultimate measure of any investment, including AI, is its return on investment.

Lead Conversion Rate: Measures the effectiveness of your AI in turning leads into customers.

Customer Lifetime Value (CLV): Helps you understand the long-term value generated from improved customer segmentation.

Sales Revenue: Track overall sales numbers to see if they align with the predictions made by your analytics tool.

Customer Engagement: Metrics like click-through rates or open rates can indicate the success of more personalized marketing campaigns.

How to Interpret Data and Make Informed Decisions

Data Analysis: Use the analytics dashboard of your AI tools to review the KPIs.

Benchmarking: Compare the performance metrics against industry standards or your past performance.

Correlation Analysis: Look for relationships between the use of AI and improvements in KPIs.

Actionable Insights: Translate the data into specific actions. If ROI is high, consider scaling the AI implementation. If lead conversion rates are low, revisit your lead scoring model.

Adjustment and Iteration: Make the necessary adjustments to your AI tools or strategies based on the data and continue to monitor performance.

By closely tracking KPIs and interpreting the data, you can make informed decisions that continually refine your sales strategy, ensuring that your investment in AI delivers the maximum impact.

Conclusion

Summary of Key Steps

Assess Current Sales Processes: Understand your existing sales funnel and identify metrics.

Identify Gaps and Opportunities: Locate areas where AI can provide the most value.

Choose the Right AI Tools: Select tools that align with your specific needs and objectives.

Implement AI in Lead Generation: Integrate AI tools to improve the quality and conversion of leads.

Leverage AI for Customer Segmentation: Use AI for more nuanced and effective customer targeting.

Utilize Predictive Analytics: Implement predictive models to forecast sales trends and customer behavior.

Measure ROI and Make Adjustments: Monitor performance metrics and adjust your strategy accordingly.

The sales landscape is evolving, and AI is at the forefront of this change. The steps outlined in this guide provide a roadmap to harness AI's power effectively. The technology is here, the tools are accessible, and the benefits are tangible. Don't let the opportunity pass you by. Take the first step in integrating AI into your sales strategy today and set your business on a path to significant growth and success.

Action Steps

1. **Evaluate Your Sales Funnel**: After reading the article by the author, start by assessing your current sales processes. Identify the key metrics you're tracking and locate gaps or inefficiencies where AI could provide value.

2. **Select Targeted AI Tools**: Based on your assessment, choose AI tools that specifically address your business's needs. Pick the tool that aligns with your objectives, whether it's lead generation, customer segmentation, or predictive analytics.

3. **Implement and Monitor**: Once you've selected the appropriate AI tools, integrate them into your sales strategy. Continuously monitor key performance indicators to measure ROI and make data-driven adjustments to your approach.

WHY INVEST IN AN ENERGY COACH?

ANNA CHOI

Nobody *needs* a coach. You only need a coach to the degree of the game you play in business or life. A coach is obviously required if you are going for the gold in the Olympics, but no coach is typically needed if you're playing in a rec league. The better question is: What game am I playing in business? If you're going for gold, continue reading.

What is an Energy Coach?

If you look up "energy coach," you may find energy healers doing Reiki, Akashic Record readings, Human Design readings, or other esoteric training. However, they don't necessarily focus on ensuring you meet your business goals.

Conversely, a business, high-performance, or mindset coach typically doesn't focus on fulfilling your soul's highest expression or unleashing your light within.

An Energy Coach for high-achieving, mindful entrepreneurs does both. They are more concrete than energy healers in delivering tangible life and business results while also ensuring you master your energy from within on a path that's aligned with your highest soul goals, like global enlightenment to benefit all humanity versus just your ego's goals of more fame, power, influence, and wealth.

An Energy Coach helps you reclaim your energy by identifying and plugging major energy leaks while adding new sources of fresh energy to feel fulfilled, happier, and at peace. You will learn tools and practices that build habits for more time, freedom, and spaciousness in life that evoke creativity and the pursuit of happiness. You will gain the courage to eliminate what is no longer working and make decisions more aligned with who you've become and where you want to be.

While you may still spend a session or two on high performance, learning a healing modality, or releasing emotional baggage in a relationship, those areas are under a bigger context of ultimate self-realization.

Three indicators you are ready

If you are searching for the most authentic expression of who you are and are willing to do whatever it takes to express that, an energy coach serving entrepreneurs may be for you.

Here are three indicators that you are ready:

1. In transition from one chapter of life to the next

One of my clients is a high-end attorney who makes great money but is burned out by her toxic coworkers, boss, and clients. Her passion for leading personal growth training as her own business was on the back burner as she survived her job.

Together, we mapped out a transition plan of what was required as a nonnegotiable in her current work to stay by a timeframe. We worked through energy drains and developed better self-care habits and boundaries that gave her the energy to easily create a new business offering to test with coworkers she had been procrastinating for years. Learning how to release energy blocks in her body on a daily basis, allowed her to take new bold steps courageously that she was paralyzed to take before.

Ultimately, she landed a huge government contract that funded her dream job as a new department within her company. She got the security and the passion to work without forgoing a stable paycheck for a new business venture!

2. Crave more energy and time freedom

Another client felt trapped in an old business she was no longer passionate about but where she had stable clientele. She was also running her newer passion business she felt she couldn't grow without the weight of the old business holding her back while taking care of her aging father.

In our work together, she identified what was draining her energy in life and business that had become tension and stress in her body. She developed a step-by-step energy action plan to slowly stop taking energy-draining activities and replace them with replenishing ones that would grow her new business. She ended up firing old clients, reducing her students, and keeping only the students she loved to work with.

The result? By releasing energetic blocks, she created a new offering in her new passion business that sold out. The courage to face her fears of firing clients and creating a new, never-been-done program gave her a huge confidence boost, refueling a future fully aligned with her vision.

3. Feeling too much pressure and responsibility as a CEO at the top

Many CEO clients are lonely at the top, having to put on a good face for their teams and family with no one to truly open up to vulnerably with their personal struggles. One client had gotten injured and could no longer work out how he wanted. Each morning he would grab his belly fat and shake his head in despair to change this with his injury. Emotionally, he felt helpless about how to best support his wife going through a failed IVF. He had no energy by end of each day to take all his responsibilities.

Through energy coaching, we pinpointed and customized unique energy exercises and moving meditations to help him love his body. He was able to deal with the pressure and responsibilities of the company with more grace and ease. Most of all, we also worked with his wife to face her fear of the IVF through releasing emotions in the body that resulted in a successful pregnancy shortly thereafter after a year of trying. In ninety days, he felt more confident in his skin again to take his shirt off in public, was at peace with his anxieties, and even landed a huge business deal as an influencer while they welcomed a new baby into the family.

A litmus test to determine if you're ready

If you're reading this, I know you're a high achiever who is up to a bigger game more aligned with your soul. You have a growth-oriented mindset and want to expand on your current experiences to manifest a bigger vision that lets your light shine brighter.

Ask yourself these questions to determine whether you know you're ready for an energy coach:

Questions to determine if you're ready for an energy coach

- Are you looking to grow?
- Do you have an outcome or goal in mind to achieve?
- Is that outcome a high priority to achieve?
- If so, in what timeframe do you want to achieve that outcome?
- Are you ready to invest time, energy, or money towards that goal?

If you can readily answer yes to most of those questions, I'd recommend interviewing energy coaches.

How to vet a coach

When finding the right coach to work with, make sure that it's a good fit by vetting them through three areas of credibility, relevance, and resonance.

A decent coach will be a sounding board, hold you accountable, help you get unstuck, and be your cheerleader. However, a stellar coach will listen deeply to understand what you can't articulate and provide the space, guidance, and tools for a transformative experience that lasts.

Credibility

Credibility goes beyond credentials to results they give their clients, plus embodying the principles they teach you to succeed. Look for congruence of what they offer, results from clients, and the energy they embody. If there's a gap, ask more questions.

Does the coach embody, live, breathe, and practice what they preach? Are the coach's words, actions, and results congruent?

For example, don't hire a health coach that is unhealthy. Don't hire a business coach who hasn't made money. Don't hire an energy coach who doesn't exude pure, bright energy.

The best energy coach embodies being an Energy Master. An

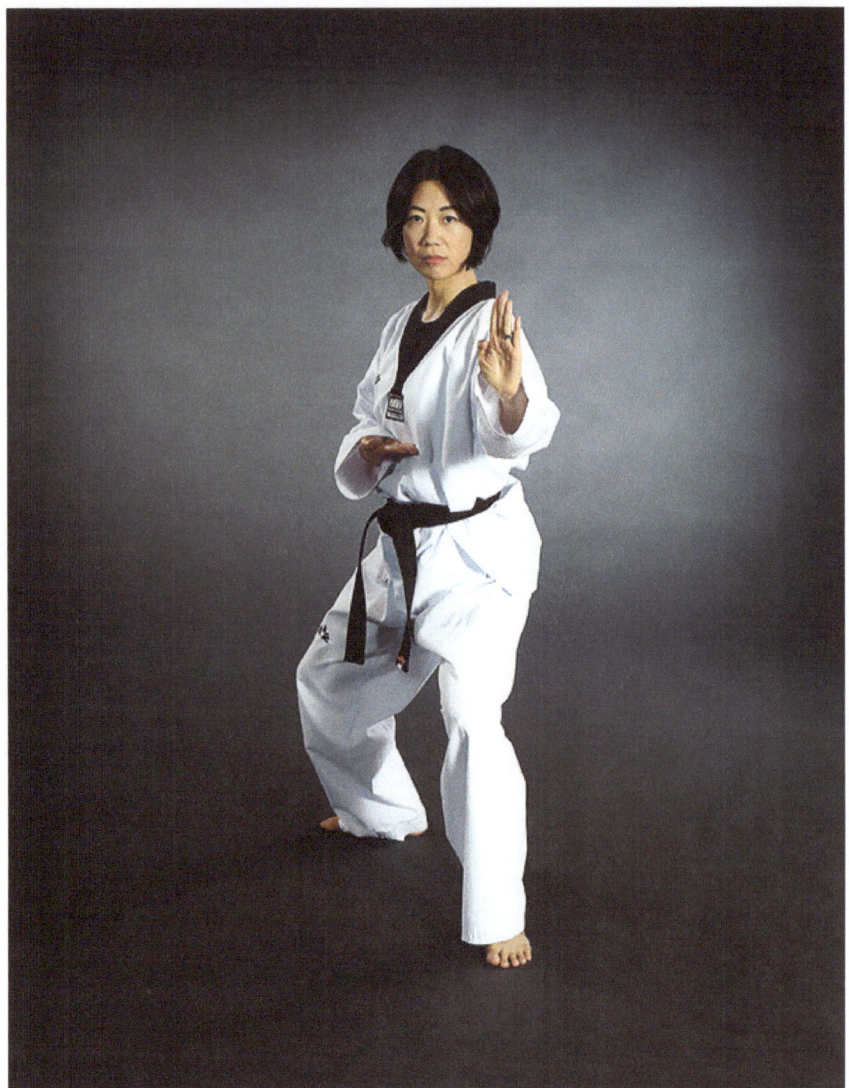

Energy Master embodies universal life force energy in daily life and exists to share these energy principles with others to widely benefit humanity.

If your goal is more energy, ask, "What have been your client results in having more energy? What was your energy like before and after coaching others in energy? What energy or self-care practices do you continue today? This allows you to get a

clear "before" and "after" picture across a specific time frame.

If hiring a business coach and revenue growth is your number one objective, you need to ask the awkward question—How much do you make?—to see if they accomplished the same level of revenue you're looking to achieve.

Also, does the coach you are considering have experience

and success in what you want coaching you on? Have they replicated their success with at least 2-3 other clients? If so, ask what those results were.

The best gauge is seeing student results that are able to do what they've done or better.

A true professional coach will already have many client success stories on their website before you even have your first inquiry call. In addition, you will see 5-star reviews on Google, LinkedIn, or other social media.

Relevance

We may often like someone, but what they offer isn't what we want. Relevance is vital in determining that you actually need what they offer.

Relevance also includes whether their expertise is aligned with your future direction. Get clear on what kind of expertise, experience, or wisdom you want to tap into. Ask what expertise they bring relevant to your vision and goals.

Before you even consider pricing or hours, the bottom line is, can they deliver what you're looking for?

Once clear on that, you should consider paying a premium to work with someone who can achieve the results in half the time. It can be a better investment than working with a newbie who will take double the time for you to achieve results, and you'll be their guinea pig client. Also, remember that return on investment (ROI) isn't just financial. ROI also includes more time, health, energy, and fulfillment.

Resonance

Next, consider whether they align with your values. Do you resonate with their energy? Aside from the "know, like, and trust factor," is there a basic chemistry?

Ideally, they will resonate on the mind, body, heart, and soul levels. There are so many coaches out there. You don't need 100% perfect alignment, but at least reach for 80% or higher. Don't settle for less just to "get the goods."

There *is* someone who has the goods *and* is a match for the type of entrepreneur you are and want to become. Trust your intuition and gut on this one. No questions need to be asked.

I've mistakenly bought a program of someone I somewhat liked enough but just wanted access to their templates and process, only to find out later their values were not the same as mine. As a result, I questioned even using the templates and processes since we were not aligned.

Questions to ask yourself when you meet them include:

- Do they believe in you and your dreams? Or do they steer you in what they think is best for you based on their own success?
- Do they ask good questions that help you gain clarity and trust yourself? Some coaches may be newer or need to deliver value upfront. They might start doling out advice immediately, which may or may not stick because you didn't discover it for yourself. The best coaches I've worked with ask questions I never even thought of, bringing an enlightening perspective that brings me to greater heights.

- Are they superb listeners? Are they intuitive enough to "get you" and read between the lines without you explicitly communicating your goals or intentions?
- Do you feel like a better person just talking to them? Whether you feel confronted, relieved, or alive, trust your gut to let you know on this one.
- Do you sense they can call you out in a way you'll be able to receive it? Some coaches are more concerned about being liked and thought of as a buddy than being a coach who will go where it's uncomfortable.

To recap, three areas to vet a business energy coach are credibility, alignment, and resonance.

Do your research. Most of these three areas can be found on their website, but if not and you feel compelled to learn more, set up a 1:1 call to interview and get to know them. If your ego mind is hungry for more money and results, it will cloud your judgment and decisions will be based on lack and fear. Instead, trust yourself and your intuition to feel whether it's a fit, even if it makes no logical sense.

As many entrepreneurs discover, business is not for the faint of

heart. If you want to catalyze the positive impact you want to make in the world, an energy coach helps you catalyze, accelerate, or magnify your dream life and vision.

They encourage you to do what feels impossible if you did it on your own. They utilize proven methodologies and systems that, ultimately, help you achieve your dreams faster with more joy, ease, and fulfillment along the way.

About the Author

Anna Choi, CEO of SolJoy. Life, energy master, taekwondo black belt, and 2x TEDx speaker, serves high-achieving, mindful entrepreneurs in the wellness industry who are athletes, creatives, and performance artists to unleash 10x their energy to catalyze a new era of humanity. Bringing 20 years of experience in entrepreneurship and trained by 2enlightened energy masters, she blends ancient wisdom, healing martial arts, and moving meditations, serving thousands of students to cause a tipping point in global enlightenment. Learn more at SolJoy.Life

MAKING A DIFFERENCE: PAUL ZELIZER'S ROAD TO SOCIAL ENTREPRENEURSHIP

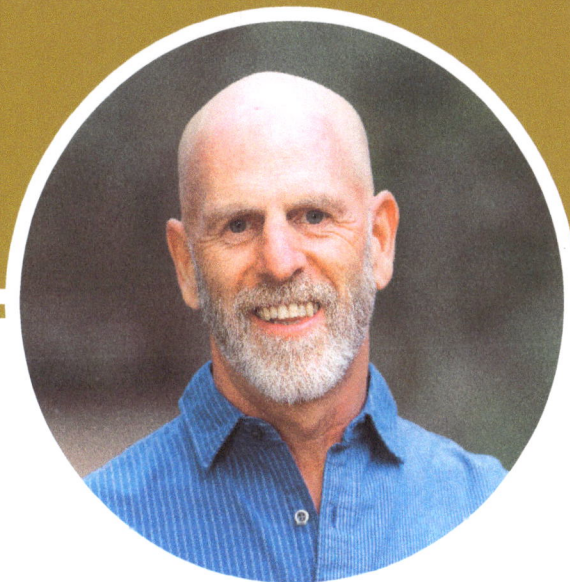

Chris O'Byrne

Welcome, Paul, and thank you for sharing your story with us.

Paul Zelizer

I've been passionate about social entrepreneurship for sixteen years, leveraging business for positive change. My first career was in the nonprofit world, but its challenges burned me out. I decided to shift my focus to businesses, a powerful force in the modern world. I've spent the last sixteen years working to make the world a better place through coaching, consulting for Impact Brands, and hosting the *Awarepreneurs* podcast, one of the longest-running social entrepreneur podcasts.

Chris O'Byrne

Let's go back to your childhood. Can you share a story of what helped you become who you are now?

Paul Zelizer

When I was around eight or nine, my dad, a tax accountant, worked for various companies, including oil and cigarette companies, even when it became known that cigarette companies were hiding data about the health risks of smoking. Despite our comfortable upper-middle-class lifestyle, he was unhappy with his job. One Saturday during that tax season, I could sense something was amiss. My dad was getting ready for work, and I asked him why he continued with a job that didn't feel right. He responded, "When you're my age, you'll do the same thing." I looked him in the eyes and firmly replied, "No, I won't."

I was grateful for our comfortable upper-middle-class life but knew something was wrong without having the words to describe it. Today, I'm a climate advocate and collaborate with climate-focused venture capitalists. I always felt disconnected from companies that conflicted with my values, which prompted my journey. My father also followed his calling, transitioning into social work, aligning with his values.

Recognizing the significance of work in our lives, even as a child, I knew the importance of aligning it with one's values, offering a sense of purpose. I've since devoted my life to unraveling this code, working with others to do the same, ensuring they can look their loved ones in the eye and say they're doing their best, even in challenging times.

Chris O'Byrne

Did you go into the nonprofit sector right out of college?

Paul Zelizer

I did. In my earlier career, I specialized in community mental health. I hold a master's degree in counseling psychology and am a licensed innovator. I worked in New Mexico, collaborating with local tribes to introduce restorative practices, such as restorative justice, in situations involving troubled youth. Our goal was to avoid sending Native American youth far away for treatment and instead focus on restorative approaches within their communities. Additionally, I worked with young men who lacked resources and needed guidance on becoming responsible fathers, offering battery intervention programs. This was my focus for the first fiteen years of my career, starting when I was just twenty.

Chris O'Byrne

Did you grow up in New Mexico?

Paul Zelizer

I'm originally from the Hudson Valley in New York, but in 1993, I relocated to New Mexico. Even today, I deeply love the outdoors and engage in activities like ultramarathons, hiking, and snowshoeing. As a young man, I was all set to move to Colorado, a typical choice for East Coasters seeking mountains. However, a close friend of mine suggested I explore New Mexico, describing it as quite a magical place. I arrived here in October 1993 and have called it home ever since.

Chris O'Byrne

As you went through your nonprofit phase, was there a defining moment when you decided to go into business for yourself?

Paul Zelizer

That's a great question, Chris. Over the past several years in my nonprofit journey, I assumed the role of executive director. I've always been an innovator, and I've come to realize that I've always been a social entrepreneur. This was particularly evident in our efforts to engage men in unique ways, as few nonprofits were thinking as innovatively about involving men in these issues. While many organizations focused on addressing problems like domestic violence or teen pregnancy, we recognized that men play a crucial role in these issues, and there was a gap in agencies or organizations taking an innovative approach. So, I decided to start one and served as the executive director for nearly eight years. Our team grew to seven members, a mix of full-time and part-time, as we strived to maintain funding in New Mexico, a wonderful but economically challenging place.

According to various economic indicators, New Mexico's economy struggled near the bottom among the fifty states. It was an enormous effort to keep the organization running, deliver high-quality work, mentor the next generation, secure funding, keep donors satisfied, and write grants while juggling the responsibilities of being a parent. I eventually reached a point of burnout, feeling overwhelmed by the workload. I knew that most economic resources and opportunities resided in the for-profit sector. At that time, terms like conscious capitalism, the B Corp movement, social entrepreneurship, and social enterprise were emerging. I felt the need to explore these avenues as I couldn't sustain the previous pace with so many responsibilities. It was a result of a severe burnout experience that prompted this shift.

Chris O'Byrne

What is the name of your business, and how did that come about?

Paul Zelizer

I'm a consultant and coach at paulzelizer.com, running Zelizer Consulting and an associated business. My podcast is called *Awarepreneurs*, a fusion of "awareness" and "entrepreneurs." My journey as a social entrepreneur has been quite messy, starting sixteen years

ago when clarity and community were scarce. I joined Twitter in 2008, initially in New Mexico, discussing conscious capitalism and values-based leadership with a small, engaged group. This led me to Google and Zappos, where I witnessed efforts to infuse more values into other corporate cultures as they celebrated becoming a billion-dollar company.

I was invited to participate, leading to robust conversations. Social media was less crowded back then. Being a connector and eager to share and learn, I joined Silicon Valley discussions about consulting, values, and purpose-driven approaches in billion-dollar companies. Sharing insights through photos, blog posts, and stories led others to seek my guidance for implementing similar strategies in their smaller businesses, which kickstarted my journey.

Chris O'Byrne

Do you primarily now work with small businesses or bigger businesses, or is it a mix?

Paul Zelizer

It's a mix. The social impact world, seen through a traditional business lens, has a diverse landscape. I discuss this on my podcast, and there are larger businesses now that prioritize social impact, like Revolution Foods. I had the opportunity to interview Kirsten Tobey, the co-founder of Revolution Foods. They bring organic, healthy food to communities, especially in areas with limited access to quality food, often referred to as food deserts. They've been operating for nearly two decades, growing into a 1,000-person company, which is a rarity in a time when few companies of that size emphasized social impact.

Even today, social entrepreneurs typically lead smaller organizations with three, seven, or twenty employees. I'm currently collaborating with a company of seventeen employees, and while there are a few with around fifty, such cases remain relatively uncommon. From a traditional business perspective, most social enterprises are on the smaller side. However, within the realm of social entrepreneurship, a fifty-person company is considered medium-sized, contrasting with how corporate America perceives such companies as tiny.

Chris O'Byrne

How would you define the term "social entrepreneur?"

Paul Zelizer

I find inspiration in the United Nations and their Sustainable Development Goals (SDGs). About two decades ago, the UN recognized the urgent need to address humanity's impact on our planet. They developed seventeen distinct SDGs, each serving as a lever to help steer us toward a sustainable future on Earth. These goals encompass a wide range of areas, from clean water, sustainable agriculture, and gender equality to clean energy sources like solar power, diversity, equity, and inclusion. I appreciate the thoughtful work of the brilliant minds behind these goals.

While these SDGs are important to me, it doesn't mean I won't engage with or interview individuals who aren't directly aligned with them. Nevertheless, the United Nations invested considerable effort into formulating these goals, and we should familiarize ourselves with them. The SDGs offer a strategic focus; concentrated efforts can significantly impact steering us toward a more sustainable existence on our planet, and that alignment deeply resonates with me.

Chris O'Byrne

Along your journey, who's been a key mentor for you?

Paul Zelizer

I'm a strong advocate for collaboration and co-learning, especially given my sixteen years of experience in the social entrepreneurship space. During this journey, I've had

the privilege of interviewing some remarkable people. One of them is Tom Vozzo, the CEO of Homeboy Industries, a network of 10,000 organizations dedicated to helping individuals reintegrate into society after prison, addressing the issue of recidivism.

Father Greg Boyle initiated this work, founded Homeboy Industries, and wrote the influential book, *Tattoos On the Heart.*

Another remarkable figure is Mohammed Younus, whose pioneering work in micro-lending transformed the lives of people in Bangladesh and Sri Lanka, enabling those living on just a dollar or two a day to access financial services when traditional banks deemed it unfeasible for nearly 40 percent of the population and didn't feel like it was worth their time or effort.

These experiences and encounters have profoundly impacted me and countless others and instilled a deep appreciation for the power of collaboration and social change.

Mohammed played a key role in developing the Grameen World Bank and pioneering micro-lending. I've had the privilege of forming a relationship with Nina Simmons, a prominent figure in US sustainability, through her work with the Bioneers Conference, which has been running for thirty-eight years. I've also connected with colleagues and friends who, like me, have been involved in social entrepreneurship for a similar duration. One such peer is my brother, Craig Zelizer, host of *The Social Change Career Podcast*, which focuses on coaching individuals seeking to make a positive impact without starting their businesses. Together with other podcast hosts and peers, we've created a valuable network for peer-to-peer learning and support.

Chris O'Byrne

I'm sure there are many other coaches and consultants in the social entrepreneur world. What is it that makes you and your business unique?

Paul Zelizer

There has been substantial growth in my journey over the years, especially since I started, and I'm grateful for that. When people ask if I have concerns about this growth, my response is a resounding "No." One significant factor is the cumulative wisdom I've gathered from the 308 episodes of my podcast. During this time, I've enjoyed interviewing 308 of the world's most intelligent and successful social entrepreneurs, who generously share their stories. This process mirrors our conversation now; I'm an open book, ready to provide insights on virtually any topic, barring confidential client information, as is the nature of interviews.

As the years have rolled by, I've developed a keen understanding of social entrepreneurs' unique challenges and pivotal moments, distinct from their more commercially oriented counterparts. The delicate balance between striving for both profit and significant social impact adds complexity. Sitting in the front row for this journey, with firsthand experience gained from interactions with some of the best minds in the world, I've garnered the knowledge and stories to offer valuable insights.

The first facet of my unique perspective is the ability to share the ideas of pioneers who have navigated the complexities of social entrepreneurship for decades. While their decisions may not be universally applicable, they provide invaluable lessons. The second aspect is the extensive network I've cultivated over the years. This network, enriched by my long tenure in the field and the reach of my podcast, allows me to assist entrepreneurs in various ways, from connecting them to potential investors to helping them find co-founders or essential team members. My network often surpasses other coaches and consultants, significantly expanding the opportunities available to my clients.

Chris O'Byrne

How long have you been doing your podcast?

Paul Zelizer

I've been at it for about six and a half years. Before that, I was a long-form blogger, posting twice a month. Google used to reward long-written content back in the day. I owe a big shout-out to my friend and mentor, Keith Carlson, who hosts the *Nurse Keith* podcast here in New Mexico. It's one of the earliest medical podcasts on the internet, addressing the challenges and meaning in the medical profession, which is no easy feat these days due to burnout and the difficult experiences faced by doctors and nurses working in public settings, such as ER rooms or clinics.

Keith, a seasoned podcaster for over nine years, encouraged me nearly eight years ago to start my podcast. At the time, I was heavily into blogging and felt like I'd just found my groove. I was hesitant, but Keith insisted, citing my relational skills and the need for a social entrepreneur in the world. During a lunch conversation, I finally gave in and agreed, realizing he was right. I launched the podcast several years ago, thanks to Keith, and it's been one of the best business decisions I've ever made.

As for what I value more, my podcasts are like my children—each unique and cherished. Tomorrow, 308 of my "children" will be out there in the world, and I look forward to telling their stories.

Chris O'Byrne

What is one of the most valuable lessons you've learned throughout your journey?

Paul Zelizer

One of the things that surprises me is how many people want to bring some positive impact into their careers but fear financial security. I love sharing stories of people who are both financially successful and making a positive difference. This desire for meaningful work resonates with me because of my dad's experience working for an oil company, like how some companies have suppressed data for profit. I see a parallel in individuals wanting their work to have meaning and purpose and make a genuine difference, contributing to a better world.

That hunger is so incredibly powerful for so many people. Some fear they can't make a lasting impact, not just through occasional volunteer projects but by integrating it into their work's core purpose. The desire for this is skyrocketing worldwide, especially with growing challenges like climate change and political turmoil. However, there's a fear that pursuing this path may jeopardize financial security for myself and my family.

I'm grateful to feature folks doing impactful work while maintaining a fulfilling lifestyle. It's not about luxury or private jets; we're climate entrepreneurs. I lead a content life, surrounded by great people, owning a home, enjoying outdoor activities, and spending time with loved ones. I

have enough to meet my needs and make a positive difference, which I can discuss with my child, sharing our commitment to addressing global challenges.

I can look them in the eye and tell them that, in this era, we're at a crossroads that is crucial for their children's survival on this planet. This is the essence of the SDGs. I'm dedicated to these goals for our family and our community.

I can do that and maintain a good quality of life. My mission is to guide those who feel a calling, showing them communities and opportunities to leverage their skills, whether in tech or healthcare, to contribute to impactful companies and initiatives. I feel grateful to be a part of that.

Chris O'Byrne

What parting words of wisdom would you like to share with us?

Paul Zelizer

First of all, let me just say thank you for having me, Chris, and thank you for doing this and for your work. I appreciate it.

Going back to the last question, two important points arise. One is the importance of doing work aligned with your values, and two is we have a mental health crisis on Earth. It's off the charts. My first career was in mental health, supported

by my master's degree and years of experience in the field. The current discussion draws on my perspective as a social entrepreneur, conversations with people developing mental health platforms, and insights from my earlier career three decades ago.

We live in a significant era, and for most adults, work consumes most of our waking hours. If you're feeling anxious and depressed because your work doesn't align with your values and purpose, let's talk. Work is where we spend the most time, even more than with family or hobbies. While some may sleep more than they work, an eight-to-twelve-hour workday is the norm for many. A full eight hours of sleep is considered a good night.

To those who haven't considered aligning their values with their work, please prioritize this conversation. It affects your mental, physical, emotional, and spiritual well-being. Start thinking about your values and how to better align them with your work for a more fulfilling life.

If you've already aligned your values with your work, thank you for your efforts. My biggest suggestion is to become part of communities that share your goals, whether it's in areas like climate, gender, solar, or regenerative agriculture. Join a community where you can learn from others and share your insights. I often tell my clients to make new and different mistakes, not the same ones repeatedly. In these poignant times, if your work is focused on making the world better, it's crucial to be in a community, sharing and learning together, as we need everyone's knowledge to drive positive change.

Chris O'Byrne

What's the best way for people to learn more about you and what you do?

Paul Zelizer

I've got a pretty unique name, Paul Zelizer, and you can find me on various social media platforms like LinkedIn and Instagram using my name. On Facebook, I'm Paul Zelizer, Business Coach. You can also visit my website, paulzelizer. com, for consulting services. If you're interested in my podcast, it's called *Awarepreneurs* and is available on all major platforms. For more details and episodes, visit awarepreneurs.com. Feel free to connect with me through these channels.

About the Author

Paul Zelizer is a seasoned business coach dedicated to supporting social entrepreneurs and impact-focused leaders in achieving their goals and creating positive change in the world. Over the past sixteen years, he's worked with over 10,000+ founders and leaders individually and in groups and he's the host of Awarepreneurs, one of the world's leading social entrepreneur podcasts. Learn more at paulzelizer. com

FROGMAN MINDFULNESS

Jon Macaskill
US Navy SEAL Commander (Ret)
Keynote Speaking
One on One Coaching
Mindfulness Teaching
www.frogmanmindfulness.com
757-619-1211

FROM CHEMIST TO MIRACLE HEALER

JOAN YUE

Dr. Joan Yue is not your typical healer; she started her career as a chemist. Known by many as the "Chemist turned Miracle Healer," Dr. Joan has a unique approach to healing that combines her scientific background with holistic practices. Her journey is a testament to the transformative power of aligning the mind, body, and spirit.

Dr. Joan's work centers on mind/body/spirit alignment, a holistic approach that aims to harmonize all aspects of one's being. This alignment is not just a philosophical concept for her; it's a practical tool. She likens her role to that of a "chiropractor of the nervous system," albeit one who operates via Zoom. Her methods aim to release repressed emotions and unblock limitations, allowing her clients to shift quickly and permanently toward peace and ease.

One of the key aspects of Dr. Joan's practice is helping people unfreeze their nervous system. In today's fast-paced world, getting caught in a cycle of stress and overthinking is easy. Dr. Joan offers a way out by releasing repressed emotions causing the stress and overthinking cycle then teaching two simple alignment tools that can be used for life. These tools help handle emotions with ease and master self-command, enabling clients to create loving relationships and a limitless dream life.

Overthinking can be a significant roadblock to achieving peace and ease in life. Dr. Joan's methods help shift people out of this mental trap. By focusing on mind/body/spirit alignment, she helps her clients tap into their inner "superpowers," allowing them to live a limitless dream with peace and ease.

Combining her scientific background with a deep understanding of holistic practices, Dr. Joan Yue offers a unique and effective approach to healing and well-being. Whether you're struggling with emotional overwhelm, chronic stress, or simply looking to improve your overall quality of life, Dr. Joan's methods offer a promising path forward. Clients are expected to make major shifts towards peace, ease, and clarity within days or weeks.

Early Life and Career: Overcoming Obstacles and Embracing Transformation

Dr. Joan Yue was born in China to parents with limited educational backgrounds—her mother had no formal education, and her father only completed elementary school. Despite these humble beginnings, Dr. Joan achieved significant professional success. However, her early life was not without challenges. She was secluded in a tool shed all day while her mother worked, as they couldn't afford a babysitter. This isolation led to deeply repressed emotions and a tremendous amount of trauma.

Dr. Joan's career trajectory took her far from that tool shed in China. In third grade, while she was still an average student, she set an intention (wrote down on a piece of paper) to come to the US (the farthest place away from China) when she grew up, even though there was no diplomatic relationship between China and the US at that time. The intention helped to start excelling in math in fourth grade and win science competitions in the middle school. She became the first one out of 150 chemistry department students to have the opportunity to come to the US at age 21 to pursue her Ph.D. in chemistry.

She became a high-powered executive at a multinational corporation, focusing primarily on numbers, formulas, and charts. At this point in her life, she had no interest in anything spiritual. Her career was demanding, and the stress from her job, compounded by the responsibilities of motherhood, took a toll on her emotional well-being.

While she was achieving career milestones, Dr. Joan was also grappling with the stress and emotional toll that came with it. She was so overwhelmed that she often found herself disconnected from her family. Her anxiety levels were extremely high, so she would respond to her children without hearing what they said. This emotional disconnect and overwhelming stress eventually led her to a breaking point.

Things got so dire that Dr. Joan checked into the emergency room, thinking she was having a heart attack. It was a panic attack, but this incident served as a wake-up call. She realized that she needed an immediate and complete change in her life, prompting her to leave her corporate job and embark on a journey for transformational tools and a more fulfilling life.

Dr. Joan Yue's early life and career are a testament to her resilience and drive. However, they also serve as a cautionary tale about the importance of emotional well-being and the dangers of neglecting it. Her journey from a neglected child in China to a high-powered executive and finally to a Miracle Healer is inspiring and profoundly instructive.

Turning Point: The Catalyst for Change and Self-Discovery

The pivotal moment in Dr. Joan Yue's life came when she found herself in the Emergency Room, convinced she was experiencing a heart attack. The physical symptoms were overwhelming, but the diagnosis revealed it was "just" a panic attack. While some might dismiss this as a less severe issue, it was a wake-up call for Dr. Joan. This incident made her realize that her current lifestyle and emotional state were unsustainable.

Following the panic attack, Dr. Joan decided to leave her high-powered executive position. She recognized that her emotional well-being had been severely compromised, and no amount of professional success was worth the toll it was taking on her health and family life. This decision wasn't just about leaving a job but seeking a complete change in her life.

Dr. Joan embarked on a journey to find the "secrets of life" and the best transformational tools available. She read all kinds of self-improvement books and did many programs but still felt stuck. It wasn't until she stumbled upon her mentor, the late Dr. Karl Wolfe, that she began to experience truly transformational shifts. Dr. Wolfe introduced her to Movement Feedback, a method that would become the cornerstone of her healing practice.

The panic attack and subsequent departure from her corporate job were the catalysts that set Dr. Joan on a new path. She wasn't seeking a spiritual awakening but a way to live an easier, more fulfilling life. Her search led her to tools and methods that transformed her life and equipped her to help others make similar transformations.

The turning point in Dr. Joan's life is a compelling narrative about the power of self-awareness and the courage it takes to make

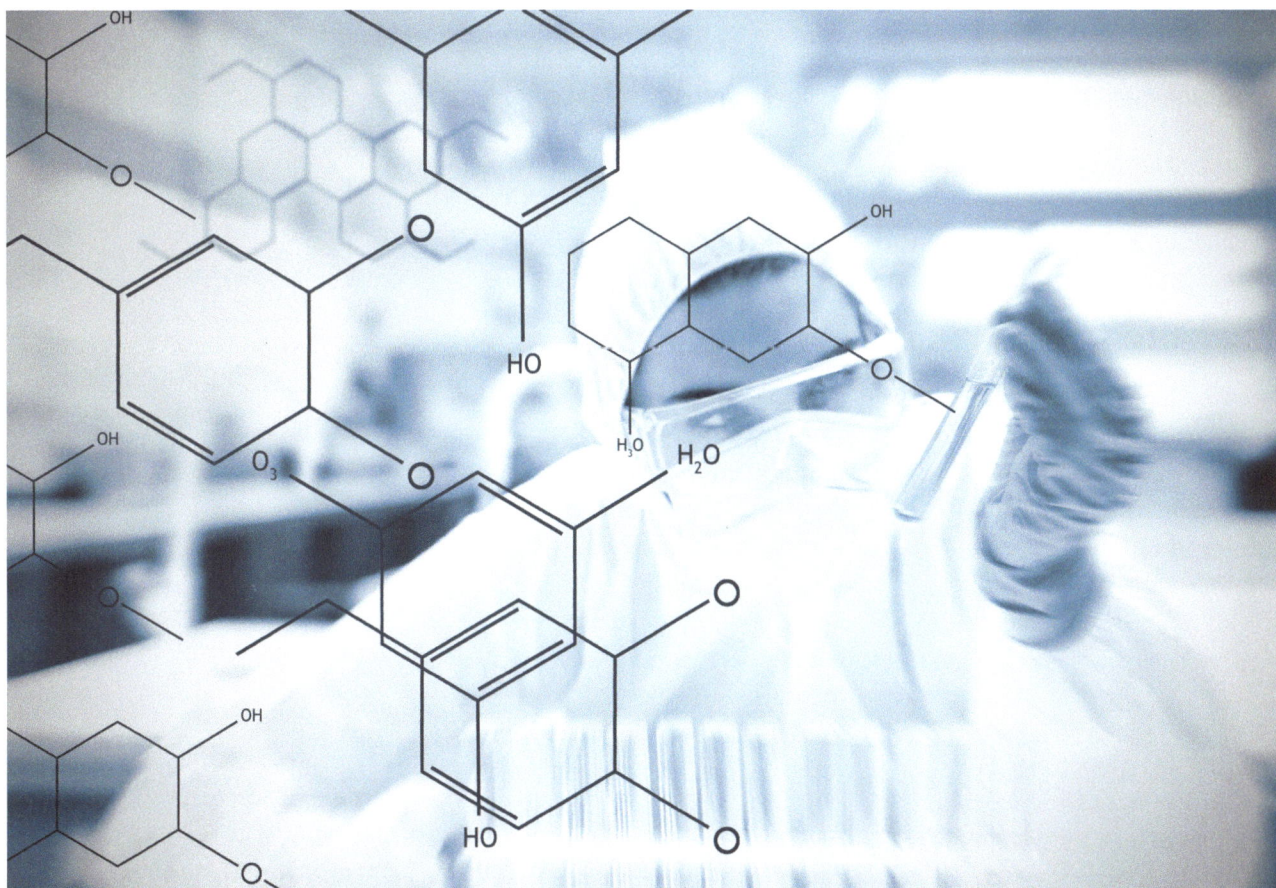

significant life changes. It's a reminder that sometimes, the most challenging moments in our lives can also be the most enlightening.

The Mentor and Method: A Paradigm Shift in Healing

As mentioned earlier, Dr. Joan Yue found a mentor in the late Dr. Karl Wolfe. Dr. Wolfe profoundly impacted Dr. Joan's life and practice because he worked with celebrities and business professionals to "add zeros" to their income. His teachings provided her with the tools she needed to make truly transformational shifts in her life and in the lives of her clients.

One of the most impactful teachings Dr. Joan received from Dr. Wolfe was the method of Movement Feedback. This technique focuses on grounding individuals in their bodies to eliminate anxiety and break free from self-sabotaging patterns. By receiving feedback on unconscious patterns revealed in her movements, Dr. Joan could let go of limitations she wasn't even aware of. This method enabled her to move forward quickly, both personally and professionally.

Movement Feedback taught Dr. Joan the importance of deeply connecting to her body. This connection allowed her to tap into her gut instinct and gain clarity and guidance on her next steps, especially when starting her coaching business and navigating difficult times. She learned that by connecting deeply to her body, she could also connect to Spirit (Infinite love or higher self) to experience daily miracles. These could range from simple things working out to opportunities arriving out of the blue.

One of the most significant benefits of Movement Feedback was its ability to help Dr. Joan eliminate anxiety. She learned to stop her constant overthinking, which had been a source of self-doubt and indecision. Her confidence skyrocketed, and she felt a sense of deep peace, like sinking into the ocean where surface-level disturbances no longer bothered her.

Transformation: A Journey from Anxiety to Abundance

Dr. Joan Yue's transformation is nothing short of remarkable. She went from being highly anxious, emotionally overwhelmed, and constantly overthinking to a state of abundance, freedom, and ease. This shift wasn't just a minor improvement but a complete overhaul of her emotional and mental well-being. She attributes this transformation to her focus on Mind/Body/Spirit alignment.

The transformation allowed Dr. Joan to live a life many aspire to, but few achieve—a life of abundance, freedom, and ease. She found happiness for no reason, a state of being that didn't rely on external circumstances. This newfound emotional freedom also had a ripple effect, positively impacting her relationships and professional endeavors.

One of the most significant outcomes of Dr. Joan's transformation was the development of a unique modality to release deeply repressed emotions. She became one of the elite few in the world who can deeply and quickly connect clients into the Quantum Field to experience profound shifts instantly. This modality has helped many of her clients release years of stuck emotions or long-term stress-related symptoms that were holding them back—all within just one session.

Dr. Joan's work is akin to a chiropractor for the nervous system, helping people unfreeze emotionally and move forward toward the limitless dreams they've desired for years. Her clients have reported experiencing "Miracle Healing," a testament to the effectiveness of her unique modality.

Dr. Joan Yue's transformation is a powerful example of how aligning the mind, body, and spirit can lead to a life of abundance and emotional freedom. Her journey also led her to create a unique healing modality, further amplifying her impact on those seeking a similar transformation.

Services Offered: A Holistic Approach to Healing and Transformation

Dr. Joan Yue describes her role as akin to a "chiropractor for the nervous system." Just as a chiropractor adjusts the spine to improve overall health, Dr. Joan works to adjust the nervous system to bring about emotional and mental well-being. She does this primarily through Zoom sessions, making her services accessible to clients worldwide.

One of the standout services Dr. Joan offers is her deep Miracle Healing, aimed at unfreezing the nervous system. This service goes deeper than conventional methods, allowing for permanent and transformational shifts. It's designed to help clients release repressed emotions and unblock limitations, enabling them to make fast and lasting changes toward peace and ease.

Unconscious limiting patterns hold many people back they may not even be aware of. Dr. Joan's services include identifying and unblocking these patterns through Movement Feedback, allowing her clients to transform completely. This is particularly beneficial for those who feel like they've hit a wall in their personal or professional lives.

Feeling stuck is a common issue, often due to a lack of clarity on how to move forward. Dr. Joan offers services that provide clear guidance on clients' next steps in areas where they feel stuck. She channels information to give them the clarity they need to navigate challenging situations or decisions.

Dr. Joan Yue's services offer a comprehensive approach to healing and transformation. From acting as a "chiropractor for the nervous system" to offering deep Miracle Healing and unblocking limiting patterns, she provides services designed to bring about profound changes in her clients' lives within days or weeks.

Why Work with Dr. Joan: Five Compelling Reasons for Transformational Change

Her deep Miracle Healing service is one of the most compelling reasons to work with Dr. Joan. Unlike conventional methods, this service goes way beyond surface-level issues to unfreeze your nervous system. It allows for permanent and truly transformational shifts, making it an invaluable resource for anyone looking to make lasting changes.

We all have unconscious patterns that hold us back, often without realizing it. Dr. Joan specializes in identifying and unblocking these limiting patterns through Movement Feedback. This service is particularly beneficial for those who feel stuck or limited in their personal or professional lives, enabling them to break free and achieve their goals.

Feeling stuck often stems from a lack of clarity. Dr. Joan provides clear guidance on your next steps when you feel stuck. She channels information to give you the clarity you need, helping you easily navigate challenging situations or decisions.

Dr. Joan teaches you how to tap into your inner "superpowers" by providing points of reference for grounding in your body. You also gain simple alignment tools to enable you to master self-command and handle emotions with ease, ultimately allowing you to make your dreams a reality.

Dr. Joan's methods help you become more accepting of your emotions, allowing you to easily handle them and be in the flow of your work and life. This mainly benefits those frequently overwhelmed or stressed, providing a pathway to emotional freedom and well-being.

Working with Dr. Joan Yue offers a comprehensive and deeply transformative experience. Her unique blend of services addresses both the symptoms and root causes of emotional and mental challenges, providing a holistic pathway to a better life.

A Pathway to Peace, Ease, and Clarity with Dr. Joan Yue

Dr. Joan Yue offers a transformative experience

that goes beyond conventional healing methods. By focusing on unfreezing the nervous system, she provides a foundational shift that allows for deep and lasting change. Her methods are particularly effective for those caught in the cycle of overthinking, a common issue that can lead to emotional and mental stagnation.

Her unique blend of services provides a comprehensive approach to well-being, from deep Miracle Healing to unblocking limiting patterns. She doesn't just address symptoms; she tackles the root causes, enabling her clients to move past their limitations and lead lives filled with peace, ease, and clarity.

Moreover, Dr. Joan's work is accessible to people worldwide through her Zoom sessions, making it easier than ever to tap into her transformative services. Whether you're struggling with emotional overwhelm, chronic stress, or simply looking to improve your overall quality of life, Dr. Joan's methods offer a promising and effective path forward. Her work will reset you back to your "factory settings," the way you were designed to live your life from the very beginning!

In a world where stress and anxiety are all too common, Dr. Joan Yue stands out as a beacon of hope and transformation. Her holistic approach to healing offers a pathway to a life of peace, ease, and clarity, making her services invaluable to anyone seeking a better, more fulfilling life.

Learn more about Dr. Joan Yue at movementfeedback.com.

Action Steps

1. **Invest in holistic well-being**: After reading the author's insights on Dr. Joan Yue, consider incorporating holistic well-being practices into your business culture. A balanced mind and body can improve decision-making and productivity, benefiting your bottom line.

2. **Identify and address limiting patterns**: The author highlights the importance of recognizing unconscious limitations that may hold your business back. Invest in coaching or workshops that focus on identifying and breaking these patterns to unlock new avenues for growth.

3. **Seek clarity for strategic planning**: The article emphasizes the value of clarity in overcoming challenges and making informed decisions. Tap into your inner guidance to gain clarity for the next steps when possible. Utilize tools or consultants that specialize in providing clear, actionable insights for your business strategy, much like Dr. Joan does for individual well-being.

www.ingramcontent.com/pod-product-compliance
Lightning Source LLC
Chambersburg PA
CBHW052053190326
41519CB00002BA/206